SECRET WARRIORS

HIDDEN HEROES OF MI6, OSS, MI9, SOE & SAS

About the Author

Charles Fraser-Smith was born in 1904 and educated at Brighton College and in Paris. In 1926 he went to Morocco to pioneer industrial missionary work. There he managed farmlands for the Morrocan Royal family, had two farms of his own and built up two orphanages.

In 1940 he returned to Britain and undertook the war work described in this book and in THE SECRET WAR OF CHARLES FRASER-SMITH.

Like another of the war's unsung heroes, Ord Wingate, he emerged from a disciplined, Biblical background, and went on to develop his own first-hand relationship with God. Whilst Wingate, with the Bible as his text book, successfully carved deep into enemy-held Burma, Fraser-Smith used the same text book in a different arena but with equal effect.

After the war he bought a farm in Devon and initiated an intensive grassland and milk production programme. Today, in his early eighties, he remains independent, sometimes controversially ahead of his times. He has an inherent reluctance to follow the crowd, particularly when it turns up a cul-de-sac. He is as busy as ever, yet still finds time to relax walking with his wife on Exmoor.

By the same author:

THE SECRET WAR OF CHARLES FRASER-SMITH
The 'Q' Gadget Wizard of World War II

With 29 photographs. (Obtainable only from the author, Dale
Cottage, Bratton Fleming, Barnstaple, Devon EX31 4SA —
£3.50 including postage).

Author's Note:
Many of the gadgets described in this book are explained
and photographed in *Secret War*, and are on display at
Bickleigh Castle Museum, Bickleigh, Devon.

Secret Warriors
Hidden Heroes of MI6, OSS, MI9, SOE and SAS

CHARLES FRASER-SMITH

with

Kevin Logan

Exeter

THE PATERNOSTER PRESS

AUSTRALIA
Bookhouse Australia Ltd.,
P.O. Box 115, Flemington Markets,
N.S.W. 2129.

SOUTH AFRICA
Oxford University Press,
P.O. Box 1141, Cape Town.

British Library Cataloguing in Publication Data

Fraser-Smith, Charles
  Secret Warriors
  1. World War, 1939–1945—Secret Service
  2. World War, 1939–1945—Personal, narratives
  I. Title
  940.54′86′410924   D810.S7

ISBN 0-85364-393-8

Photoset in Great Britain by
Ann Buchan (Typesetters), Surrey and printed for
The Paternoster Press Ltd., 3 Mount Radford
Crescent, Exeter, EX2 4JW by
Cox & Wyman Limited, Reading.

Contents

Preface

This is a factual record of those World War II agents, officers and men, who were supplied with equipment by my secret supplies department. It tells of the men and women who used my gadgets and equipment, and those who made them. For the lone secret agent, evader or escaper, individual heroism of the highest order was needed. They were not spurred on by team spirit, as those who fought *en masse*. No war correspondent scribbled in attendance. Nothing was seen. There were no headlines as those brave soloists faced unimaginable terror and danger, not even knowing if their work was recognized or used.

This then, is my tribute to those who remained in the shadows of the limelight; the hidden heroes, many of whose deeds went unpublished, not only during the war, but up until recent times, because of the thirty-year clause in the Official Secrets Act. Although I am into my eighties, I still thrill at the small contribution I was able to make, equipping our undercover lads and girls to cope with their risky business.

Until recently I avoided war books, having heard and seen enough between 1939 and 1945. It was not until the autumn of 1977, on a visit to my daughter in New York, that I was drawn back to those days of war. My son-in-law, Alan Williams, knowing the thirty-year silence clause to be up, pursued me with the tenacity of a British bulldog. I was eventually bullied into the nearest library and allowed to retreat only with a platoon of war volumes and with orders to read and digest. My assault on this mountain of military literature brought me first to the 'Big Guns', the statesmen and generals, all thundering out their own exploits. Next came the historians, who with their careful war research had manufactured more mature publications.

But where were the annals of the real heroes; the silent legion whose dangerously-obtained intelligence had provided their superiors with their spectacular successes? Our bedecked and charismatic leaders seldom seem to pass down the kudos and praise which the lower, but vital, ranks so richly deserve. Perhaps it is only when the 'small fry' are drawn in that a more accurate picture of the whole develops.

May this book help us to appreciate more fully the debt which we owe to the small man. In rank, he may be small. In retrospect, he is a giant.

Charles Fraser-Smith

1

The beginning

Winston Churchill listened intently. The hour was at its darkest. Dunkirk had come and gone. The Americans and the Russians had not yet arrived, and any suggestion that offered a glimmer of promise took precedence even over the ever-present cigar. The man to whom Churchill was listening was Hugh Dalton, and the content and manner of his words produced the nearest approximation to a smile that could be conjured from the Prime Minister's weary features. The cigar had been long cold when Churchill eventually spoke.

'Hugh, go ahead. Set Europe ablaze.'

That abrupt order brought into being one of the most unorthdox and thrilling operations of World War II. It sent Dalton away from No. 10 Downing Street as head of what was to become known as the Special Operations Executive (SOE). His brief: to train and dispatch agents across the Channel who, in turn, would establish clandestine Resistance groups to harass the enemy by every possible means. The highest seal of approval was stamped on a licence to subvert and cause general chaos from within the efficient German machine.

Dalton, like Churchill, refused to be dominated by the need for defensive strategy. Retaliation was the only conceivable option for lonely Britain. Every effort, however minute, must be made to tie down the giant enemy just as the Lilliputian web of cotton enmeshed Gulliver. War from within would involve sabotage of factories, demolition of electricity pylons, disruption of communications and transport, derailment of troop trains, misdirection of goods wagons by changing destination labels, and the strategic use of the time-bomb. This then was how Dalton planned to set the beleaguered Continent ablaze.

Incredibly, he and his fledgling department were almost extinguished before they even saw the enemy. Within days of his meeting with the Prime Minister, Dalton was locked in a war of survival against the Foreign Office and its Secret Service department, MI6. The rigid orthodoxy of the regular armed forces also tried to strait-jacket him. Had time been his ally, Dalton might have employed diplomacy to fend off the opposition. But Germany, having blitzed through France, Belgium and north into Holland, Denmark and Norway, was now poised within a clear day's view of England. SOE had to be assembled hurriedly. There was no British precedent for such a clandestine group; it was so unlike the regular services, with their standard hierarchies and their bureaucratic mandarins and protocol. Dalton was cast as the heretic, and his philosophy and strategy anathematized. With no proven working manual and few experienced men, teething troubles were many, providing the threatened Establishment with welcome ammunition with which to eliminate these upstart amateurs. MI6, who considered SOE an unhelpful and unwanted rival, provided the biggest opposition. Actually, MI6 were in no position to criticize, employing as they were, albeit ignorantly, a fair proportion of sub-agents of the Soviet Secret

Service in the persons of Philby and Co. SOE networks were certainly penetrated, but not to the extent suffered by MI6 before, during and after the war.

Dalton's headquarters at 64 Baker Street, were continually frustrated by jealousy and distrust and the solution was far from elementary, as the street's more illustrious non-conformist, Sherlock Holmes, might have deduced. But whereas Holmes had his bumbling Watson, Dalton was about to secure as a colleague the highly-efficient Major General Sir Collin Gubbins, who arrived with the dignified and recognizable pedigree of KCMG, DSO and MC.

Gubbins, shortish, neat and trim with twinkling grey eyes and a tooth-brush moustache, applied a soothing diplomatic balm with the full force of his magnetic personality and quiet humour. A Scot, he had only recently returned from a highly original raid in Norway and nothing could quench his determination to make SOE just as successful. With Gubbins came an amazing rainbow of personnel. His recruitment drive produced a dubious selection of underworld characters. Who better to teach his agents how to crack a safe, counterfeit German currency and break-and-enter with the minimum of fuss? Most enlisted criminals displayed keen patriotism, especially when their job contract included a reduction of sentence. The Major General also brought in insurance investigators as sabotage consultants. They had had more knowledge than most in this subject, though from the more practical side.

While all this was happening, I too was being taken on, in a less romantic department, in the innocuous guise of a Ministry of Supply civil servant. My orders were to keep the secret network of Britain supplied with whatever special equipment and gadgetry they needed. My main master was MI6, but MI9, SOE and later the Special Air Service (SAS), used me whenever necessary.

With the wholesale drafting of civilians, an untrained recruit was often unable to assume the bearing of a trained officer, and consequently acted – and looked – out of place, much to the disgust of the regular wallahs. They had me measured for a major's uniform, '. . . just to give added authority, old chap'. But knowing that the directors of the firms with which I dealt did not respect the regulars because of their lack of business acumen, I declined in favour of my civvie suit. I found that the 300 firms with which I dealt rose much more readily to the challenge and fun of producing gadgets when they were dealing with a civilian like themselves.

Uniforms often had a strange and unhelpful influence on people's personalities, as did the training which normally went with them. It produced a stereotyped military attitude which, though an asset in the regular ranks, was a positive liability in secret work. A dose of disciplined square-bashing and a military bearing would have been no asset to Nancy Wake, for instance, as she sat opposite an over-attentive fellow passenger in a train *en route* to Marseilles. Above her head, in the luggage rack, was her case full of Resistance contraband. The passenger–a German, a sixth sense told her–obviously found her attractive, and she fought for inner calm while gazing placidly at the passing countryside.

'It is very cold, is it not?' The passenger's French was perfect-perhaps too perfect. It was time for a test.

'We French people,' she began innocently, 'don't have fuel any longer to heat our trains as you do in

Germany. That's why we always travel in these skiing clothes.'

'They suit you.' He smiled, without denying her innuendo. She forced herself to return the smile. If he was a German, he was just the man to help carry her luggage through the barrier of police checks which would be inevitable at the destination. The young German continued to flirt with her until they drew into Marseilles station when he proposed that they make a date for the following day. Nancy readily agreed after seeing the platform dotted with German police. She later learned that station security was at red alert following the explosion of a Resistance bomb.

'Allow me,' the German said as she stretched for her case. At the barrier the police took an interest until, with an arrogant gesture, her fellow passenger produced a Gestapo identity card and the security officials fell back in respect.

Nancy, married to Henri Fiocco, a rich Marseilles industrialist, was responsible for helping hundreds of agents and POWs to escape from France. After the war she received decorations from three countries. Her civilian attitudes were a positive bonus on another occasion when, climbing a steep hill with her husband and two disguised British evaders, she turned a corner to find Gestapo officers chatting around their parked Mercedes Benz. Nancy at once set off at a run— *towards* the officers! She reached their car, panting out:

'This is too much!'

'What is?' asked one of the puzzled German officers.

'All you lucky men in that lovely car and I'm walking up this steep hill!'

Her cheek amused the Géstapo. 'Would Mademoiselle like us to drive her home?'

'Of course!' With that she jumped into the car, to the horror of the trio behind her. They later found Nancy sitting quietly at home.

'Much quicker and easier than walking,' she grinned. 'And oh dear, if only you could have seen your faces when I was driven off!' And she collapsed into helpless laughter.

When it came to recruiting agents, the criteria were a level head, steady nerves and one hundred per cent discretion. Many prospective agents failed the initial interview when tested on the first three rules of the SOE. They were told to look at everything they saw, take in everything they heard and never ask about anything that did not directly concern them –'Observe, remember, keep your mouth shut'. A number of motives drove them to work for the SOE. Some were pure patriots wanting to fight in a righteous cause. Others detested everything that Hitler and his Third Reich represented. A few enjoyed the demands that the job made on personal initiative and action, and others came seeking adventure, excitement or just the chance to stare danger in the face.

'It is more interesting to live a short adventurous life and do something, than to live long and safe and do little or nothing.' This was the motto for many. One of the characters in John Buchan's *Greenmantle* declares, 'What's life, anyhow? It isn't such an almighty lot to give up, provided you get a good price on the deal.' Many would have agreed that to live and die having achieved little apart from one's own personal ambitions would be empty and useless. Life was for living, with a capital 'L'.

I liked the *joie de vivre* of René Duchez, an

interior decorator who supplied information and maps of the Atlantic Wall in the months before D-Day. He used much of my secret equipment, such as miniature cameras. The Gestapo arrived at his home in Quistreham one day to interrogate him, only to find Madame Duchez apparently trying to pacify a client who was raving about work mishandled by her husband. The 'client' was promptly thrown out of the house by the Germans so that the premises could be searched. The front door was slammed shut and the client's anger turned into instant joy, tainted only by the terrible criticisms he had levelled at his own good workmanship.

A man who liked to test himself against the enemy was Gilbert Michael of Caen. The Germans regularly press-ganged French hostages on to trains in order to dissuade the French Resistance from blowing them up. They would seize any local men who happened to be near the railway station, force them on to the train and give them special passes for their return journey. Michael was able to discover the movement of troop trains through his home town, and would arrange to be on hand whenever hostages were required. Time and again he was able to travel in comfort, at the Germans' expense and through prohibited zones, quietly noting the progress of the Atlantic Wall. He also memorized regimental identification signs and the numbers of men on the move. At Cherbourg there was generally a half-day wait for the return train, which gave him time to survey the harbour and its many military installations. On returning home he would swiftly pass on relevant information to the Resistance to be forwarded to London.

The professionalism and incredible effectiveness of our agents stemmed from their early training in the Scottish Highlands in and around a granite castle near Arisaig and their finishing school at Lord Montagu's stately home at Beaulieu. The first essential was to ensure a prospective agent's physical fitness, and then came judo, karate and the use of ropes, up, down, round and across all manner of obstacles. Training for women was particularly tough. One instructor – as much of a dictator as Hitler – met his match when a member of the 'fairer sex' decided that it was time for a little democracy. Her fellow pupils watched with a professional eye as she matched the instructor, hold for hold, in judo. There was sheer delight when the instructor was eventually forced to retire, having been debagged down to his underpants!

These women were not only efficient but totally discreet. I remember one in particular. I had rung for a car, and a Buick arrived. We sped through Whitehall as though it were White City and I formed the uncomfortable impression that the lady driver was no sedate English rose. In fact, she turned out to be Belgian. Things had been getting a little too hot at home and she had popped over 'for a rest'. And that was the only thing I ever got from her – that and the kaleidoscopic blur of London which left me pining for my usual chauffeuse with her healthy respect for speed limits.

The French Section of SOE under Maurice Buckmaster trained and sent out thirty-nine women. Fifteen were captured, and of these only three survived the concentration camps. All were in their twenties and had personal motives to hit back at the Germans, who had hurt them or their loved ones during the initial invasion.

Occupied countries provided the majority of SOE agents. The French, Belgians, Poles, Czechs,

Norwegians, Dutch and Danes all had scores to settle with the Nazis. But at the beginning of World War II we were hopelessly unprepared in the field of intelligence and resistance and the final cost to life and the economy in the five years it took to subdue Germany was inexcusable. The setting up of SOE should have been done sooner. I trust that today a similar set-up is on hand in case of another war.

Once SOE had become established, and the initial mistrust of other secret agencies had been dispelled, 64 Baker Street expanded at an astonishing rate. By February 1942, SOE had requisitioned St Michaels House from Marks and Spencer, together with adjacent property – Berkeley, Chiltern and Orchard Courts and Bicknell Mansions – and had scores of agents networked throughout Europe. Many others were based in Cairo, which was the centre for all intelligence work in Africa, the Middle East and the Balkans. There was a Jewish SOE agency known as 'The Friends', under David Ben Gurion and Dr Weizman. There was also the Haganah, the Jewish secret army which was later followed by the Mossad, Israel's secret intelligence service, all of whom used my equipment from time to time. The Israelis were particularly fond of my small radio sets which could be dismantled quickly and the pieces hidden. They also liked my line in miniature transmitters which operated with the cord of an electric shaver acting as a long-range antenna. They even used my Yardley soap, not to hide maps as the European agents did, but to secrete explosives and small detonators.

Once agents were trained to their peak they had to be equipped with the 'Rolls-Royce' version of every conceivable item. That was where I came in.

Each of our men had to be dressed according to local custom, even down to the correct buttons and material. Shirts, socks, footwear – all had to tally with those worn by the local people among whom they would be living. Authentic items of dress came from many sources. A warehouse in Oxford Circus produced genuine French suits and dresses. Messrs Rigby and Peller supplied corsets, underwear and super French knickers. I always found it amusing to be calling on Madame Rigby at 12, South Molton Street, W1. A Northampton manufacturer provided the required continental-style boots and shoes. Running a wardrobe for our agents was a mammoth task in itself, and everything had to be precise. A wrong stitch or shoelace would have meant the hell of torture followed by a firing squad. I used to spend hours around Paddington's second-hand stalls and shops, hunting for 'Made in France' clothes. Suitcases and briefcases were particular headaches until we arranged to relieve all Frenchmen arriving in England of their luggage. None objected, especially when each received a brand new English replacement. Lost property depots were veritable Aladdin's caves, and when the owners arrived they were easily persuaded to swop old for new.

Ration and identity cards were a further problem, mainly because the Vichy government insisted on changing them periodically. The Free French in the UK were invaluable here. Within hours, they would get all the necessary information from their contacts at home so that when our agents were dropped, all their documents tallied with the area in which they were to work.

We were often called upon to help the Resistance Movement with sabotage, a word derived from *sabot*, the French word for clog. In the Industrial Revolution, dissenting French workers would introduce one of their clogs into the new-fangled mechanism; invariably the machines came out of the encounter rather the worse for wear. We managed to devise a replacement for the clog in World War II – abrasive grease. It looked and felt like any normal lubrication, but it could reduce pistons, bearings and all moving parts of machinery to inefficiency and eventually to rattling rubbish. Of course it was easier to supply agents with the recipe rather than produce and transport the grease ourselves. A mixture of Vaseline and sand was quite acceptable in an emergency.

The most effective material for sabotage that we supplied was plastic explosive (PE). This 'plasticine' could be moulded into any shape, and pressed into cracks, holes and corners. It only exploded when fused, burned or hit. It was excellent for filling in the joints between railway lines. Saboteurs could be miles away when the Germans arrived to blow themselves up. With a few artistic touches, PE could merge with any surroundings, whether as a cobblestone or a cow pat.

The requirements of agents were endless. One woman asked for Elizabeth Arden make-up and lipstick, indicating her preference for type and shade, 'Just to keep up my spirits and morale.' There was little time for casings to be remoulded with French markings, so all English signs were erased. Some agents wanted pep pills, such as benzedrine. Others objected to this, but it was essential that a man going into action should be able to draw on maximum resources when necessary, so we camouflaged the packet, naming them 'Energy Tablets'. Cyanide 'L' pills were another difficult personal problem. If the pill was found on an agent it was as good as a confession, and there would be a slow day-by-day torture, and possibly death. We decided to supply ingenious rings which would house the pill for those who wanted to take them. The 'L' pill covering was insoluble and could be held in the mouth. It had to be crushed between the teeth. If swallowed whole it passed through the body without harm.

Perhaps the most important item for an agent was an efficient watch. Accurate timing of operations was often a matter of life and death, so only the best would do. All watches that I supplied came from Switzerland, whose people I believed to be among the most intelligent and hard-working in the world. The Swiss refused to produce anything which was not of the best quality. They had a national genius for precision, value for money and honesty which permeated the whole nation. They expressed the divine truth that wealth alone does not bring happiness; but that righteousness and beauty of environment are priorities for true satisfaction. Their Rolex, Omega and Rotary watches were the ones I supplied to the agents.

One of my best customers was Ben Cowburn, an oil technician from Lancashire, who was one of our earliest SOE Baker Street agents. He specialized in sabotage and brought off one of the most successful coups of the war. A batch of brand-new express engines arrived at the locomotive depot in Troyes and were considered vital to the Germans for transporting troops, equipment and ammunition just after the D-Day landings. On hearing the news, Ben rounded up his small band of demolition experts and set to work. The explosions turned the depot into a cross between a plumber's dump and a scrap metal yard, and the Gestapo immediately rounded up every French railway worker in sight for interrogation and retribution. However, when we supplied time-bombs they were always clearly marked to show their English origin, and one bomb had been left undetonated for the Gestapo and the pro-German French to find. They deduced that it was an outside professional job by a British agent and released the local Frenchmen.

An amusing sequel followed. The Germans needed materials for large barriers to prevent repetition of the explosive incident. The supply job went to Pierre Mulsant, one of Cowburn's saboteurs! He made sure he charged top prices!

Cowburn completed four long spells in France, and his meticulous planning enabled many an evader to make it back across the channel. He was intrigued by my maps on rag tissue paper, silk or nylon. He liked to use my trouser-button compass. Once we issued him with French Gauloise cigarettes, made in London in their well-known blue and white packets. On receiving his first packet, he spotted that they were fractionally longer than the real thing, which we immediately rectified. Our facsimiles of French match boxes, however, were given his ten-out-of-ten pass mark.

He often used my small curved spade, that fitted the calf of the leg, for the purpose of burying secret equipment. This spade was also fixed on the leg of a flying suit so that, on landing, one's parachute and other equipment could be buried immediately.

When I was asked by SOE to come up with some sort of portable trowel, I rang Dr W. E. Shewell-Cooper, for whom I had done some horticultural research work, and asked him to put me on to a trowel firm. He was a renowned expert on horticulture and used to advise the Queen Mother on her gardens; also the author of numerous books on gardening subjects. He told me who to contact – Harding Ltd. I asked the firm to develop a special curved trowel that could fit inside a sock, to be strapped to the calf of the leg. It was to be made without handles, but with a hand-sized slot through which to grip it.

Having equipped our agents, ensured their fitness for action, and even continentalized their dentistry, we now had to get them across that small stretch of channel and drop them into occupied territory. And that is another incredible mixture of heroics, obstacles and sheer determination and courage.

2

SOE takes off

Above the door in an isolated corner of Newmarket Racecourse the notice warned 'Jockeys Only'. Yet no jockey ever entered through its portals, and if one had he would have been totally perplexed. A man in casual civvies browsing through music manuscripts would have given him an inquiring look. If by some far-fetched coincidence the jockey had hit on a certain combination of words, the music man might have snapped into brisk military action, opened the door behind his desk and ushered the rider into a mysterious world. He would have entered a large room, wallpapered with aerial photographs and maps, weather charts and signals. The language of its occupants would have seemed no better than gobbledegook, as they talked into a battery of telephones about lambs, parcels, customers and 'The Organization'.

All this might have happened – but never did. The preoccupied musician was, in fact, a highly professional security 'front' man. He was the 're-ceptionist' for a small RAF unit which·ran the first 'delivery service' for SOE, known to the pilots only as 'The Organization'. 'Lambs', 'parcels' and 'customers' were, of course, codewords for agents in transit. As an added security measure, the unit's Whitley Flight of three aircraft was based on the far side of the Heath, three miles away in the care of

Squadron Leader P. Knowles. He had been given the task of delivering agents by air, after sea landings became too dangerous on the well-guarded French coasts.

The first 'set down and pick up' mission was given to Flight Lieutenant 'Whippy' Nesbitt Dufort. He could put his plane down in impossible places, and had earned his nick-name doing so. He had been mesmerizing the crowd at Hendon air pageant with one of his acrobatic routines and was returning to his home base. With several miles still to go, the plane's engine spluttered and fell silent. Dufort's stomach sank in unison with the plane, while his eyes searched anxiously for a flat piece of earth. Fighting to control his steep downward glide, he eventually spotted a postage stamp of a field, which, as it gradually appeared larger, became a faint possibility. He came in low over a high fence and dropped his plane on to the uneven grass. It was only after he had bumped to a halt and climbed out of the cockpit that his nerve broke. A few yards away half a ton of African rhino was thundering towards him, bent on mischief. He took flight, this time without his plane, and leaped over a nearby fence. Whippy had put down smack in the middle of Whipsnade Zoo!

There were many dramatic incidents during Dufort's numerous SOE trips. In 1942 *The Times* reported him missing, believed to have been shot down and killed over occupied France. Two months to the day after his crash, he walked into his home-base mess, casually sat down and ordered his evening meal.

The SOE delivery service itself had desperate moments. It also had its inter-departmental enemies in addition to the real ones across the

Channel. Most of the opposition came from the high personage of Air Marshal 'Bomber' Harris, who claimed that the delivery service was a waste of his valuable aircraft. SOE's incessant delivery demands always outstripped the unit's ability to supply, but it often seemed an easier proposition to hijack a Luftwaffe squadron than to extract additional flying machines from Bomber Command. This was especially true later in the war when the highly questionable carpet-bombing of cities and their civilian populations came into vogue. SOE seethed over the terrible waste. The thousand bomber raids, in which tens of thousands of British and American aircrew died over Germany, killed hundreds of thousands of civilians and flattened hundreds of square miles of city centres and houses. But to what purpose? Had the planes been used to ferry the backlog of agents and supplies, real and lasting damage could have been inflicted on the enemy. Efficient Resistance groups could cause panic and chaos. A few well-placed bombs by saboteurs could cripple an industry, telephone communications, a rail terminal or a road network; that was much more effective than blasting civilians and their homes into blood and rubble. The outcome was that instead of our bombing hampering enemy war production and demoralizing the people, it had just the opposite effect.

General Eisenhower credited SOE and its activities with shortening the war by at least nine months.

'Give me one SOE agent,' he said, 'he is worth fifteen divisions.'

It sounds like one of those exaggerated Americanisms. But not from Ike. He chose his words honestly, and the General could have cited many an occasion when that statement might have been an understatement. Perhaps he was thinking, for instance, of Hervé, an agent in Evreux, Northern France. It was D-Day + 15, and a Panzer corps was speeding towards a bridge over the Eure river to prevent a breakthrough from an Allied beachhead. The RAF had already failed to knock out the bridge, and Eisenhower eventually called in SOE. Hervé, a fearless agent, borrowed the local postman's uniform and bicycle and concealed a powerful explosive charge beneath the mail. The German sentries, with their indoctrinated sense of good order, knew that 'the mail must go through'; they even gave Hervé an escort across the bridge. As they reached the centre span, Hervé detonated the bomb and blew the bridge, the soldiers and himself to pieces. Minutes later the Panzers drew up in a confused melée making an easy target for a previously alerted squadron of Typhoons. The SOE could have placed many more 'Hervés' behind enemy lines, had the planes been made available. However, soon after it outgrew its Newmarket Headquarters and moved (in March 1942) to Tempsford in Bedfordshire, SOE managed to win over a high-ranking ally. He was Wing Commander F. Edward Yeo Thomas, GC, MC, an incredible Resistance leader and one of the toughest characters that the war had produced. The pre-war Yeo Thomas was a French couturier and a director of the Parisian House of Molyneux, but his war record was a complete contrast. He was with the RAF in Paris when France collapsed, and eventually escaped in the last cargo boat bound for Milford Haven. After various frustrations he was drafted into the SOE, but not until he had accused the Air Ministry of misusing his talents and experience and had threatened to have the issue raised in Parliament.

Yeo Thomas's first mission was to return to France with 'Colonel Passey', the code-name for André Dewavrin, head of Deuxième Bureau (The French Secret Service). Their mission was to seek out and co-ordinate various French Resistance groups which had splintered because of their political differences. My role as usual was to give them the best equipment and documents available. 'Passey' especially treasured my small signet ring with its swivel top and space for one cyanide pill. He, more than most, could not afford to be taken alive by the Gestapo. Their task was satisfactorily completed – except in the case of *Front Nationale*, (the French Communist Resistance), which refused to co-operate, preferring to take orders only from Moscow. Having united the majority of resistance work in France, Yeo Thomas returned to launch an intensive drive for equipment of every description. The equipment demands came pouring in to me through one of his colleagues, Squadron Leader C J Whitehead, MC. It started with a telephone call from Room 527, Hotel Victoria, London. An hour or so later, Whitehead was ringing again, this time from the Airborne Corps headquarters at Moorpark, Rickmansworth. Within two hours he was calling from Camp Twenty, right out in the country at Wilton Park, with still more orders. And so it went on and on. First on order were silent pistols, automatics, daggers, hand grenades, explosives and general ammunition. Next it would be torches, French money and dozens of underpant-to-windjacket wardrobes. Then it was a shipping order of concentrated food tablets, benzedrine and other drugs. The equipment and materials I supplied were stockpiled at Tempsford in an old dilapidated-looking barn – a good camouflage. Inside, reinforced concrete protected the stores. From there, agents were equipped and flown to their dropping zones across the channel.

The hunt for extra aircraft still ended in a blank wall erected by Air Marshal Harris. All that Yeo Thomas did or said merely echoed back to him from the wall of obstinacy, and there seemed to be no solution to the transport problem. Wasted days stretched into months of lost opportunity. Yeo Thomas, in utter frustration, finally decided to quit. For a courageous officer, the decision tasted of failure, and when his superior, Major General Sir E. D. Swinton, offered an alternative, Yeo Thomas grasped it with both hands. The alternative was to tell Churchill.

'I can give you five minutes,' said the Prime Minister, leaving the Wing Commander standing as if to underline the time limit. Months of frustration and anger lent an urgency to an otherwise calm and cool narrative of the brave men and women risking torture and death, and the appalling lack of aircraft to drop vital supplies.

The time limit expired. 'Sit down,' ordered Churchill. It was nearly an hour later when Yeo Thomas walked out into Whitehall, hardly able to believe the promises that he had heard. But within forty-eight hours twenty-two Halifaxes, twelve Liberators, thirty-six Stirlings, six Albermarles, and several small 'pickup' planes had arrived with a promise of more to come. The delivery service had at last taken off – and not a day too soon. D-Day was on the drawing board, though, of course, only Churchill and his select band knew that.

The delivery service landed 443 agents in France, and returned with 635 passengers. Four planes were shot down and a few crashed or got bogged down. Only six pilots were lost.

3

Tricks of the trade

Britain's inter-departmental rivalry was a mere angelic tiff when set against the devilish conflict in the enemy camp. The two major German Secret Service networks literally waged a war within a war, and each was the other's biggest enemy. On one side was the Abwehr, the old school, headed by Admiral Wilhelm Canaris. Facing them were the zealots of Hitler's Nazi SD, who would have goose-stepped over a precipice had their 'god' so dictated. Canaris found himself in the impossible position of wanting a German victory but not if it meant domination by Hitler and his ideology.

General Ludwig Beck, Chief of the German General Staff, was in the same dilemma. When he found out about the colossal scale of the slaughter carried out by Hitler's special units in Poland, he declared to a Lutheran pastor, 'Hitler is one of the most evil men ever to walk the face of the earth.' In July 1942 after again hearing of the atrocities done during the advance into Russia, Beck in rage exploded, 'What has this swine Hitler done to our country?'

Admiral Canaris often resolved his own dilemma by feeding false information to his unwanted leader, and that must have been worth battalions to the Allies. It is amazing that the ex-corporal survived in power as long as he did, with the combined intelligence work of the Allies and that of some of his own side working against him.

The British Intelligence Services took a wicked delight in leading Adolf and his High Command up any and every path but the right one. One memorable ruse stemmed from a telephone call to my office in the Ministy of Supply, (my department was coded CT6, – Clothing and Textiles Department 6 for the forces – to link me with my main masters MI6, who had their headquarters next door).

'Hello, CT6? I hear you know something about dowsing, old chap.' It was Naval Intelligence who, at that time, were desperate for any ideas to reverse the demoralizing failure in the U-boat war. They apparently wanted to investigate the dowser's gift of locating subterranean minerals and the possibility of applying it to submarines. They had heard that I had used the services of a dowser before the war when my Moroccan farm ran dry.

'Just give me a little time,' I replied, 'and I'll dig one up for you.'

The Ministry of Agriculture later sent me round a Mr. Visick who was not only a wizard with the usual Y-shaped rod but claimed also to locate his quarry by means of a pendulum predictor over a map. He was quickly vetted by Security and then dispatched to Naval Intelligence with my compliments.

The investigation into the possible dowsing of U-boats in the Atlantic came to nothing, as was expected, and our failure under the sea was eventually rectified when more serious scientific research revealed that German U-boats were able to dive below 600 feet. This had previously been thought to be an impossibility, and our depth charges had consequently been wasted with wrong settings. My 'detective work' in uncovering Mr.

Visick did not, however, go unused. We knew, via our intelligence network, that Hitler and some of his immediate staff were dabblers in the occult. So Naval Intelligence leaked the rumour that the pendulum-swinging method was our secret weapon in the sudden increased successes in locating and destroying the underwater enemy. Within days, the Germans had diverted some of their best brains to form a Pendulum Intelligence Team under Kapitan Hans Roeder. It was months before the truth about our little trick dawned. By that time the U-boat War had swung in our favour.

Dowsing is not actually an occult practice. It is an inherent gift of sensitivity possessed by some people to detect the presence of underground reserves of water and minerals. But Hitler, submerged in his religion of astrology and occultism, with *Mein Kampf* as his prophetic bible, could not tell the difference. Had he bothered to read the real Bible, Adolf might have made a better job of World War II. One of my favourite authors, the prophet Isaiah, wrote some good sense in the world's best seller and could have put the German leader right.

'You felt sure of yourself in your evil. . . disaster will come upon you and none of your charms or spells can stop it. . .'

Another of my favourite writers, St. Paul, put it even more succinctly:

'What a man sows, that will he reap.' Apparently, Hitler did just that.

Magic of a more recognizable kind was one of the Allies' greatest weapons, especialy in the deceptive hands of illusionist Jasper Maskelyne. It was one of the greatest thrills of the war for me to provide my boyhood hero with the gadgets and equipment needed for his astonishing war wizardry. Some of his magic had the top men scratching their heads. One of them was FBI chief J. Edgar Hoover. He was standing by a small lake in Canada early in the war when a fleet of British battleships suddenly materialized out of thin air. 'How on earth did they get so far inland?' Hoover demanded to know.

Maskelyne had rigged mirrors by the lakeside to produce this magnificent deception, using toy battleships. It was just one of many magic moments of World War II in which he created false fleets, guns, tanks, and non-existent armies. He used models for many of his illusions and I was one of his supply men producing special materials from which he constructed his deceptions.

At the beginning of the war, news of Jasper's magic met with little enthusiasm. He had obtained a commission in the Royal Engineers and was full of ideas for deceiving the enemy. The top brass, however, thought the theatre of war should not be trivialized by parlour tricks, and for a long time chose to ignore Maskelyne's highly expert knowledge, passed down from previous generations of illusionists. It was Lord Gort, the magician's Commander in Chief, who eventually gave him his long overdue 'audition'.

'Maskelyne, I want a machine-gun post in a field,' he ordered, 'and try a little of this camouflage you keep talking about.'

A few days later, the C-in-C, together with his retinue, arrived at the field appointed for the trial. Nobody was there. Nothing could be seen. Lord Gort decided that Maskelyne had misunderstood the arrangements – a black mark already! Gort and his staff set off across the field to check the next meadow.

'Halt, who goes there?' the command rang out of

thin air. Two steps later Lord Gort found himself looking down the business end of a machine-gun. The Maskelyne magic had won its first fan and he was soon heading for the big-time.

The illusionist's live military debut was made in Egypt where General Wavell wanted to know whether Maskelyne could 'Hey presto' tanks into ordinary army trucks. Wavell insisted that the transformation must be so simple that it could be made overnight. Jasper requisitioned a spare tank and within a few hours had a surprise ready for the general. The tank looked exactly like a lorry, with its dummy driver's cab, wooden sides and a painted hood. Wavell smiled with anticipation of the coming fun. His general's eye view of the desert campaign had detected a large Italian offensive building up, with its focus on Alexandria and Cairo. With a small convoy of Jasper's 'tricks', he now felt that he could prick this dangerous balloon before it went up.

The few tanks at Wavell's disposal were 'magicked' into lorries one night. Each was fitted with a length of chain at the rear, and these ingeniously dragged behind to erase the caterpillar tracks and replace them with tyre marks. The few 'lorries' moved ahead in what looked like a disorderly group of unarmed transport to a weak point not far from the Italian lines. Wavell then made a feint attack elsewhere with three uncamouflaged tanks supported by a convoy of ordinary lorries which Maskelyne had camouflaged to look like tanks. When the enemy's air reconnaissance reported a large tank force approaching, the Italians redirected their own tanks to repel them. It was then that Wavell struck with his small camouflaged tank force, smashing through from behind and enveloping the enemy's huge dumps of fuel and supplies. Without these, the Italians were sent scuttling back to Tobruk and Tripoli as fast as they could get away. Maskelyne's magic had conjured a sensational victory out of almost certain defeat. At the time, Wavell's troops had been outnumbered five to one!

Maskelyne's work rapidly became a feature of many campaigns. When Montgomery took over the desert war, Jasper's illusions were used to draw enemy bombing away from vital targets. He used his expertise to create dummy oil jetties, ships, and rail heads complete with authentic looking lines. They proved irresistible to the enemy aircraft who subsequently wasted thousands of bombs while more valuable targets were left intact. Maskelyne always ensured that, even if the enemy did not get value for their efforts, the pilots and air reconnaissance teams did. He rigged small explosive charges to his dummy installations together with quantities of highly inflammable material, just to make sure that the explosive effects looked right. Of course, with a few overnight repairs, the dummies could be renewed for the next wave of bombs. Walls were patched and the punctures in the inflatable ships repaired.

Enemy proof of the success of Maskelyne's camouflage work is seen in the diary of Heinz Schmidt, Rommel's aid-de-camp. He records that Rommel was called 'The Desert Fox', but, when Montgomery arrived, a new Fox had appeared in the Desert.

Like Rommel, Montgomery used cunning deception and bluff to disguise strength or lack of equipment, but there was a difference in technique. Where Rommel disguised lorries to look like tanks to conceal his weakness, Montgomery transformed tanks into harmless-looking transport vehicles to conceal his strength.

Schmidt also relates how they were deceived by a pipeline being laid to the south. Its completion was deliberately prolonged, and it looked certain that no attack would take place until it was finished.

Montgomery totally outfoxed them, and that was the commencement of their defeat at El Alamein.

Perhaps Maskelyne's greatest spectacular was in June 1944 when he helped to convince the Germans that the Allied landings would be at the Pas de Calais. In that green and pleasant part of England opposite Calais, Maskelyne constructed false airfields with dummy aircraft and military equipment. The Germans were convinced that England's invasion would be aimed across this short stretch of channel and accordingly concentrated their crack troops in that region. Even when Allied forces arrived on the beaches of Normandy, the enemy dismissed it merely as a diversionary exercise, and this gave our lads invaluable time to establish themselves firmly on the beaches and inland.

Maskelyne's spare time was devoted to lecturing pilots and specialized groups of officers on the principles of escape and evasion. He used many of my gadgets, but also had a few of his own to pull out of his magic hat. One simple idea dreamed up by Jasper was a burnt match with an inlaid magnetized needle. This would be carried in the pockets of agents or pilots going on dangerous missions. If caught, enemy guards would hardly bother about prisoners idly tossing a used match into a puddle of water. They would never dream that the prisoners were in fact taking compass bearings in readiness for a possible escape. Jasper also invented a chainsaw, with diamond-shaped links made of tooled steel and chromium plated. It passed acceptably as a decorative watch or key chain but could in fact cut through iron or wood. A refined development of this was made. It was a Gigli saw used in brain surgery. This was so fine and flexible that it could easily be concealed from sight in cap badges and in ordinary shoe or bootlaces.

A post-war development of this saw is interesting. Passing a stand at the Devon Agricultural Show I saw a Frenchman selling pocket saws. He admitted the idea came to him from a wartime shoelace. He was very intrigued to find I had introduced it.

Jasper's special fountain pen proved very nasty for any Gestapo officer who tried to catch an agent or evader. The pen fired a small but overpowering squirt of tear gas which temporarily blinded those who became too inquisitive.

Britain was at her most deceptive in a section known as the Double Cross Committee. The story of Hans Hansen is a good illustration. It was a glorious day for the German Abwehr when their golden boy, Hans, became the first of their field agents to be awarded the Iron Cross First Class. Records captured after the war revealed that Hansen, based in England, was graded as one of the enemy's 'Superstars'. They considered his weather reports and information on airfields and other installations to be of great value. He had fulfilled all his early promise when, at the outbreak of war, the young Dane had become an ardent Nazi and offered himself for the cause of the Party. He was trained and dropped with his AFU wireless set near Salisbury on September 3rd 1940.

The Germans prized his topographical and local observations so much that they kept him well endowed with funds. Hans would, for instance, radio the Abwehr asking for £4,000 for a special job. They would reply at the end of his next broadcast instructing him to board a certain number bus at a certain place and time and sit next to a well-dressed gentleman reading *The Times*. After a few minutes, Hansen was to ask, 'Anything of interest happening in the news?' Passwords would then be exchanged.

'You may have it,' his contact would say, offering him the newspaper. 'I'm getting off at the next stop.'

Inside, Hansen would find the necessary money in Bank of England notes fixed between inside pages that had been pasted together.

Towards the end of the war, Hansen, who was happily married to an English girl, had so pleased his masters that he was awarded the German Iron Cross in gold. He was the pride of the German Secret Service and their captured records classed him as an unsurpassable agent who had survived for five years in England.

He was also the pride of the British Secret Service! Hans Hansen was, in fact, one of our most successful double agents. His recruitment came as a direct result of breaking the Abwehr cipher. In 1940 Scotsman Sir David Petrie became Chief of MI8 dealing with the surveillance of the complex German wireless traffic. Under his command, Hugh Redwald Trevor Roper, a twenty-five-year old historian, and his colleague, a Major A. Gill, managed to crack the Abwehr code. But it was a slow laborious task, and results were often too late for effective counteraction. Later a copy of the top secret German Enigma encoding and decoding machine began to be built up at Bletchley Park, the government's cryptography and interception head-quarters, and I was kept busy meeting demands for all sorts of electrical and mechanical paraphernalia. We eventually completed the machine, and throughout the war the Germans never suspected that we had it. Possession of the Enigma meant that we knew at once most of the secret orders of the German High Command; this gave MI6 and MI5 information upon which they could act. We often had advance warning of German agents being sent to Britain, and a 'reception party' could be laid on for them. Most of these agents, on being arrested, realized that becoming a double agent was prefer-able to being shot as a spy. Hans Hansen was one of these, though his conversion came about not through fear, but after long discussion with the Secret Service intellectuals.

To handle these 'gifts' which the Germans kept parachuting to us, the Double Cross (XX) Com-mittee of twenty men was set up under the direction of Sir John Masterman. The double agents were used to transmit back to Germany what the Allies wanted them to know. Of course, much of the transmitted information had to be accurate, and some of it even useful, otherwise the captured agents would have lost the trust of their former masters.

The members of the XX Committee were given high priority in the secret war, but they rarely asked for financial assistance – donations from the Abwehr, wrapped in copies of The Times, covered most of their running expenses.

Deception was an everyday essential in other areas of the war. SOE Naval Units could not have survived without a good line in disguises. Edward Clark, a master mariner with the Belfast Steamship Company, discovered this for himself a few days after receiving a signal from the Admiralty. He was ordered to report to Portsmouth and take command of HMS *Tarana* with the rank of Lieutenant Commander. Hoping for a reasonable command, he anxiously flipped through the pages of the Navy List. But of HMS *Tarana* there was no sign. Thoroughly mystified, he packed his bags and obediently reported for duty. His heart took a crash dive when he was shown aboard a grubby little foreign trawler and the mystery deepened when he discovered that his junior officers appeared to possess no special naval qualifications and were also in the middle of concealing high-calibre weapons on board. It was not until the arrival of a high-ranking Admiralty officer that all was revealed.

Clark learned that he and his command were to join a 'ferry service' to run between the Rock of Gibraltar and occupied France. His cargo would be human 'parcels' and his contact on the Rock would be a man called 'Sunday'. This, in fact, was Donald Darling, a burly agent of MI9, the section which dealt with escape and evasion. Commander Clark was to know nothing of MI9, SOE or any other Secret Service that used his ferry, but he certainly fell easily into the undercover nature of his work.

One of his first assignments in 1941 was to pick up a 'parcel' from the southern French coast, which, when unpacked, turned out to be Squadron Leader (later Air-Commodore) Whitney Straight, the celebrated American racing driver. Straight had been shot down over Le Havre and after weeks of adventurous trekking had reached the South of France where he made contact with SOE and MI9 agents. As a result, the ferry was alerted.

Clark gave the order to cast off, and the *Tarana*, boasting the respectable black hull and grey superstructure of a British war vessel, slipped smoothly out of Gibraltar flying the White Ensign. As the Rock dipped below the horizon all hands were called on deck. First, the shape of the funnel was altered. Uniforms were then changed and foreign ropes and gear were strewn haphazardly about the deck. While all this was going on, other crew members were slung from the rails giving the *Tarana* a different coat of paint. A foreign flag was finally hoisted. Whitney Straight was quite surprised to be rescued by what looked like a Portuguese fishing vessel, and even more so when, during the return trip, he was press-ganged into menial deck-scrubbing as the *Tarana* was once more transformed at night into a ship-shape British naval vessel before entering Gibraltar.

The *Tarana* and her sisters on the ferry service played a vital role in returning our valuable men to the war effort after they had either escaped from prison camps or evaded capture on being shot down. Many of the ferry passengers were quite famous, such as Captain Peter Churchill or the French General Kleeburg. One night the *Tarana* arrived back in Gibraltar having had plenty of help with her seagoing transformation. On board were more than 100 agents, escapers or evaders. She was certainly no ship that died of shame. She ended the war with a nice finish to her paintwork plus the *Croix de Guerre* with bronze palm – one of the very few vessels to be so honoured. Her master received the *Croix de Guerre* with gold star, as did her three officers, Sowden, Warren and Whiting. Her six ratings were awarded the *Croix de Guerre* with silver star by an appreciative French Government. Strangely, no British decorations were ever awarded to them.

The SOE Naval Units were equally successful elsewhere, especially on the coasts of Brittany where similar disguises were donned by the ferry vessels. The ferry men became quite expert in returning our stranded airmen. On one night thirty-four British pilots were brought back, and on another occasion one airman was back in England only nine hours after parachuting from his doomed plane over Northern France.

This expertise was due to the tremendous efficiency of the Breton 'Ferry Service' under the leadership of Captain Frank Slocum RN with assistance from Daniel Lomenech, who knew every inlet of his native Brittany. We also provided a few gadgets to improve night time pick-ups, such as my luminous ping-pong balls. These consisted of two, clear perspex, hollow semi-spheres painted on the inside with a special luminous compound and fused together. Agents could use them to lay a trail for ease of return to a waiting boat, or ferrymen could use them for making their presence known to agents or evaders in hiding. The Resistance also proved a great help in our naval rescue missions. Unobtrusively, they would watch Germans laying beach mines and then plot a path between them to provide us with safe landing beaches for the rest of the occupation.

Trickery and disguise were very often the only means of hitting back at the enemy during the early part of the war. We fought the might of Germany alone – waiting with hope for the United States to realize that we could not fight the Free World's war on our own. There were a few individual Americans, however, who could not wait to come to our aid. One of them was young Devereaux Rochester.

4

From America – without much love

Devereaux Rochester had not long come of age and this thoroughly modern American miss of 1939 was determined to open each and every room of life and examine their exciting contents. Since childhood she had yearned for what she regarded as her 'very own Independence Day' and there was now no parent, no finishing school headmistress, and no other authority to bar her way – or so she thought. September of her coming-out year produced one stubborn door that was to test to the utmost the strength of her resolve.

'War,' her Greek holiday host pontificated, 'is not an appropriate occupation for a mere slip of a girl.' This infuriating patriarch insisted that she be a good girl and accept passage home on the next available ship. Miss Rochester had no intention of accepting such a dull prospect.

'Hello! it's Dev!' She had overcome the spaghetti telephone lines of a war-torn Europe to reach her mother in Paris. 'I'm coming to join you so I can help the war effort.'

Mrs Rochester was not amused, and told her wilful daughter so in unmistakable language. The newly independent Devereaux then tried another key in a door that was threatening to lock her away from a world which seemed to be growing more exciting by the hour.

'Excuse me, I need a visa for France. Can you help?' The American Embassy official hardly glanced at her application before promptly reserving her a cabin on the first west-bound boat leaving Athens – not for Paris but for New York. Furthermore, the official detailed an escort to 'help her' arrive safely on board. Escape was impossible. Her only hope of freedom now would be at Marseilles, the first port of call, where she had to transfer to a States-bound liner. But on arrival, she was met by another Embassy 'warder' at the foot of the gangwalk.

'Oh, but I must go to Paris,' she pleaded.

'Sorry, Miss,' replied the equally determined US official. 'All American citizens must be repatriated. No exceptions.'

'But I'm not prepared for a voyage.' Dev's alert mind sensed a way out. 'I must go and get some toilet requisites and sanitary towels.'

The last two words, unmentionable in 1939, put her escort into a blush of confusion.

'I'll only be an hour,' smiled Dev. Whereupon she escaped by taxi to catch the first available train for Paris. That was Dev Rochester's first lesson in evasion – a gift that she was to perfect as one of our first American recruits to SOE. Not long after she reached Paris, giving her mother a near apoplexy, the Germans arrived in town. Dev was soon unable to tolerate the occupation restrictions, and escaped to Switzerland with the aid of contacts in the newly formed French Underground. It was her successful negotiation of the border country that first attracted the attention of our local SOE agents. Her experience was too valuable to ignore. And they had no difficulty recruiting this adventure-loving girl as an undercover border courier. Within a year, she had proved so useful and talented that she was released for special training at our school for agents in the Western Highlands of Scotland.

Here also her abilities and quick wits gained her top marks. The training nights, wearing cork-smeared make-up and lobbing hand grenades, reached their climax in a graduation exercise.

'Rochester,' said the commanding officer. 'You have one hour to retrieve a bottle, and if we see you do it, you're a dead agent.'

She was handed a map and compass and given the location. She did not have to be told that the area would be infested with the colonel's radio-linked spies. Forty-five minutes later, having camouflaged herself, she spotted the bottle anchored in a fast-flowing Highland river. She also spotted an ally. A local lad out walking his dog was only too happy to play cops and robbers with her and retrieve the loot. Then he offered to show her a short cut, which quickly brought her to the rear of the colonel's shooting lodge. As she approached, the sound of his voice drifted out of a half-open window.

'Where the devil can she be?' Exasperation was tinged with anxiety. 'The silly fool must have fallen into the river and been swept away.' The colonel was getting ready to order out a rescue party when Dev tapped on the window, held up the bottle and smiled sweetly.

'There's still a minute to go, Colonel.'

Dev lived up to her early promise and became one of our most valuable agents back in France, where she survived the war with honour. She was an unwitting pathfinder to the main US force which followed rather less willingly in her wake after Pearl Harbour. The Japanese attack bombarded the isolationists in America out of their complacency, and it also brought their newly formed spy agencies into an (initially) uneasy partnership with us.

At the beginning of the European phase of the war, America had no equivalent to our MI6 and no experience of our Special Operations Executive. Their nearest approach to undercover work seemed to be a notice near the White House:

NO PARKING – US SECRET SERVICE ONLY

A photograph of this would have made an amusing Christmas card to send to our security-minded secret sections, hidden away all over London in ordinary commercial buildings. MI6, for example, had its headquarters in an antiquated office block called Minimax House; its front door brass simply declared, 'Government Communications Bureau'.

The fall of France caused many Americans to examine their own readiness for war. As a consequence, President Roosevelt sent his special emissary, Bill Donovan, to study our intelligence system and also to evaluate our chances of survival. He was an ideal choice for the job. He had won every American decoration for gallantry in the First World War, and was quick to appreciate the invaluable work we were doing, and what it meant for America. Donovan declared during an address back in Philadelphia: 'Our view has been wrong. We have been talking of aid to Britain, as if that country were a beggar at our gate. In point of fact, Britain has so far been our shield.'

Donovan also discovered that the American Intelligence set-up needed a radical revision after comparing it with the organisation and techniques of British Intelligence. He took an in-depth look at our SOE resistance and sabotage work, our psychological and political warfare, and realized that America would also have to employ similar unconventional means if she were ever to join the war. We carefully briefed him on our successes and also on the teething troubles and mistakes, especially those resulting from inter-departmental clashes. He then returned to the States. With a magnificent effort, and against enormous opposition from the political, military and naval hierarchy, he established the Office of Strategic Service (OSS) – the equivalent of our SOE.

Not all Americans were so teachable. This was evident to us even before Pearl Harbour. Our newly installed German Enigma code machine gave us a few days' warning that the Japanese were about to attack. But American Intelligence refused to believe that we could have learned of such a secret. When the day of December 6th 1941 was prematurely darkened with the smoke of fires from thousands of bombs, we found it incredibly difficult to avoid an 'I told you so' attitude. We continued to meet with stubborn opposition from Americans who refused to learn from our mistakes. Regular service chiefs were the main culprits. Admiral King, for instance, who was the Commander-in-Chief of the US Atlantic Fleet, once said, 'We prefer to learn our own lessons. We have plenty of ships with which to do so.'

A similar attitude prevailed in North Africa and even as late as the Omaha Beach operation on D-Day, and also in the Ardennes, all of which disasters were due to military chiefs rejecting British Intelligence advice. Although Britain and the Commonwealth had twice as many in combat against Germany, America with her money and weapons insisted on taking control of the European invasion, even though repeatedly it had been proved that she lacked practical experience. Perhaps the greatest tragedy was the reluctance of Roosevelt and his advisers to take our intelligence advice concerning Stalin. We knew Stalin for the monster that he was, and our judgement was backed by centuries of European knowledge and experience. What a price the Americans, with us, have had to pay since that ruinous carve-up of Europe!

We did, however, win quite a few converts – General Patton was one. Along with other army chiefs, he considered MI9 and SOE initially to be a waste of military energy and money. But then his son-in-law was taken prisoner of war. From then on we were kept busy supplying his troops with our full range of escape and evasion tricks. Many Americans also attended our MI9 Escaping and Evasion Training School at Highgate, known as Intelligence School 9 (IS9). They were familiarized with my gadgets and evasion techniques and had the pick of a library of World War I escape books which I had bought in bulk from Penguin Books, Foyles and Woolworths.

Directly after Pearl Harbour I called on the London-based American Military Attaché, George Peabody (later General) at his HQ in Grosvenor Square. He was one of my many supply contacts. He once had a US bomber deliver a consignment of miniature camera/radio sets for me. King George VI had previously sent one of these, a gift from Roosevelt, down to my department thinking it would be of use. My visit to Peabody was a tit-for-tat operation. I viewed his secret hardware and I took him a choice selection of our gadgets. He was intrigued to find that we had reduced the camera/

radio to half its original size. He was also interested in our tiny compasses which were, by this time, being incorporated in most military and airforce uniforms. If captured, a soldier or airman could flick off a 'doctored' button or insignia and take a compass bearing in readiness for escape. Peabody was delighted when I accepted a comprehensive range of US buttons and insignia for alteration.

Shortly afterwards there followed what can be best described as a multi-gadget swop shop. The Americans flew a bomber over loaded with secret equipment, and we staged an intriguing exhibition trying to 'outgadget' each other. I immediately pounced on one of their inventions – nylon. It was just the material we needed for our range of European maps which we regularly secreted in agent's shaving brushes, tobacco pipes and other personal possessions. Apparently, Japan had provided the US market with silk but Pearl Harbour had put a stop to trade. Necessity had then mothered the invention of this synthetic silk and it was given the appropriate acronym of Nasty You Lousy Old Nippon – (NYLON).

The comments swopped during the exhibition were almost as interesting as the exchange of gadgets. When the First Lord of the Admiralty arrived together with Lord Mountbatten, the Air Force Chief groaned, 'Kaput! We've lost all hope of priority – the Senior Service will now grab the lot.'

The Americans had one supreme advantage over our Secret Service. They began with new and highly original minds. In many ways, our intelligence sections were hampered by the 'old boy network'. We were riddled with 'regulars' and the stereotyped officer class. Many were career officers whose conventional minds and fear of missing promotion made them totally unsuitable for the risks of unconventional warfare. We badly needed the type of people being recruited by the Americans – ex-detectives, businessmen with inventive minds, customs men who knew all the dodges, and even fiction writers. Eventually, the overwhelming demand for more agents brought outsiders in to British intelligence, including Ian Fleming, the creator of James Bond. The man behind 007 often borrowed my gadgets to show them off to his friends in Naval Intelligence. However, in some of his books Fleming got things a little mixed up. In collusion with Dunlop, I had provided golf balls for our POWs. They contained compasses, printing ink for forging documents and other material to enhance escape attempts. But I had to ensure that those balls looked and behaved exactly like ordinary ones. When Ian Fleming pinched the idea for diamond smuggling in one of his plots, his method was anything but foolproof. The golf balls would have bounced in the most peculiar way if used in real life. Fleming, however, was the type we needed. Thankfully, the war brought in all sorts of geniuses.

Following Pearl Harbour and our multi-gadget swop shop, Bill Donovan set up a full liaison between SOE and his OSS. Sparks flew with the early friction. Many Americans were anti-British and refused our experience and advice. Those who welcomed it were accused by the remaining isolationists of 'selling out to the Limeys'. Others accused Britain of sinister and ulterior motives in pursuing the partnership. The hope of setting up a fully integrated American/British organization at first seemed to be an impossible dream. We often had to sit and watch with frustration as the

Americans made the same mistakes as the fledgling SOE had made earlier. Differences in outlook, characteristics and even language phraseology did not exactly help either. But as the war progressed we gradually learned to trust, and work, with each other, especially out in the field where differences could prove fatal. By the end of the war, our combined intelligence was so good that we were able to tell the defeated enemy the precise location of every German regiment so that they could be told to surrender.

It is to be hoped that there is a British subversive warfare department today in close co-operation with an American equivalent. Russia mimics the Fatherland of yesteryear in its military build-up and has an unhealthy obsession with nationalizing neighbouring properties. I wonder sometimes just how much priority our intelligence services are given. The Information Research Department set up by the Foreign Office to counteract Communist propaganda in this country was closed down in 1977 by the Labour government of the day. The same government refused to reduce the number of KGB agents allowed to pose in this country as diplomats and trade officials. Fortunately, their successors expelled 105 *en masse*. We have also been hoodwinked into employing several KGB agents in high positions. The recent revelations of this shocked the nation and made us wonder: how many more are still in Her Majesty's Service? Could we cope with Russia? Can we keep up the pace when the KGB spends fifty times more than MI6 and MI5 put together?

'The victor in war is he who is best informed.'

5

Co-operation – at last!

Ask a hundred people why we won the war, and you might collect almost as many answers. Some would suggest that it was won by inspiring leadership, or the steadfast British Tommy, not forgetting his Commonwealth and American counterparts. Others would suggest the atom bomb, though that really put the finishing touches to a victory that was already ours. The older folk might state dogmatically: 'God was with us and against Hitler.' And being one of that generation I would endorse that one hundred per cent. But to the list of answers I would add one more: partnership.

To put it simply: we outwitted the enemy more times than they foxed us, because we 'got it together' more efficiently than did the opposition. Certainly there was friction, as we have already seen. And of course our problems in working together were on occasions more like tooth extractions than mere teething troubles. But while the Abwehr and the Nazi SD were at each other's throats, we were at least together in the same harness and pulling towards an agreed goal, even if we did snap at each other *en route*.

The reign of terror that was launched against the enemy after the devastation of Dunkirk is a vivid illustration of this partnership. It involved Britain's three armed forces. When the Americans joined in the fray and witnessed our combined operations in action, they immediately created a carbon copy among their own forces. The reign of terror began on October 11th, 1941. That was the dateline on a top priority signal which arrived for one of Roosevelt's guests in the White House. It read:

P.M. TO LORD LOUIS MOUNTBATTEN.
WE WANT YOU HERE AT ONCE. THERE
IS SOMETHING YOU WILL FIND OF THE
HIGHEST INTEREST.

Mountbatten flew to Chequers where Churchill informed him that he was to be Adviser on Combined Operations. His job was, in the Prime Minister's words, 'to use the coast of Britain not as a bastion of defence [which many thought the only sensible course of action] but as a spring-board for attack.' He was to use the combined talents of all forces to terrorize and confuse the enemy so that they would not know from where the next attack was coming.

Lieutenant Colonel Dudley Clarke must be credited with the original thinking behind the special raiding parties. In his early fighting days he had personally experienced the ferocious harassment of Boer War guerilla fighters, and recollected that it took a quarter of a million troops to contain a mere 25,000 South African farmers. Churchill had also been in the South African war as a soldier, prisoner and escaper. Dudley Clarke therefore submitted his guerilla ideas to the Prime Minister via Sir John Dill of the Imperial General Staff. Four days later Churchill personally instructed Dudley Clarke to mount a raid across the Channel, and before the end of a week the first British commando unit was being formed. The last Britons to have been cast in the rôle of guerillas were probably those in Boadicea's reign, and consequently the first half dozen operations were experimentally primitive and understandably inefficient. Sea-sick soliders, for instance, landed to face the enemy feeling like death warmed up, and when Mountbatten arrived to take charge, his first advice was to call in the sailor/soldier marines.

For us at the Ministry of Supply almost every raid was an education. Mountbatten's commandos kept us busy meeting demands for an ever-increasing sophistication in equipment and weaponry. One of the many hundreds of problems was that of the German guard dogs. We experimented with fifty different substances, including aniseed, to mislead the Dobermanns in case of a chase. A more conventional order involved Wilkinson Sword providing me with 250,000 commando knives with lethal seven-inch blades of carbon steel, set into diamond cross-sections and crowned with brass knuckle grips. They had a black nickel finish and bore no identification marks. An efficient cosh was another essential. Sand in a sock was effective in an emergency; but the spring-coil strap with weighted ball, normally provided in tube trains for standing passengers to hang on to, proved an excellent bludgeon for temporarily disposing of the enemy. More gruesome was the consignment of lengths of cheese wire with wooden toggles at either end, which we had made up. They were a quick and silent way to dispatch a troublesome guard.

The greatest hazard of a raid was not so much the enemy as the unknown terrain at landing points. Many early commando units were unceremoniously washed up on French beaches like flotsam and jetsam. Water depth, jagged rocks, sinking sand and other unknown hazards caused delay and even disaster. Reconaissance gear had to be supplied for measuring beach inclinations and contours, and for the examination of the sea floor. In complicated conditions we supplied commando pathfinder units with inflatable suits which could also be used for underwater inspection. Fixed to a suit were the necessary measuring instruments and also a matt-white slate board and chinagraph pencil so that notes could be made under water. At the beginning of these raids, the list of equipment needed seemed endless. Requests ranged from special intricate items of weaponry down to miniature knuckle-dusters. Climbing gear of every type was also needed to negotiate every conceivable nook and cranny. As we became more professional, cosmetic grease paint replaced burnt cork or mud daubs. Tins of solidified fuel were produced for cooking quick snacks. We even invented self-heating tins of soup.

The early commando had to be taught everything – field craft, concealment and infiltration. One of the greatest landing hazards was the activity of seagulls with their hungry curiosity about anything that moved. Circling and wheeling seagulls alerted the enemy to many a commando raid until the boffins came up with a simple solution. The commandos' 'square-bashing' gait was replaced with 'field-shuffling' as they were taught to mimic the slow, plodding movement of cows. The men also had to practise boarding canoes at the stern and launching out of them sideways without capsizing. These were no parlour tricks at night on a choppy sea, especially when rigged out with inflatable suits and all their appendages. Commandos survived only through initiative and originality. They had to be one hundred per cent volunteers, knowing that they might only have a fifty per cent chance of surviving any operation. Their fitness had to be that of marathon runners and their endurance in the field was often incredible.

After the D-Day Landings, Lance Corporal Selby and Trooper Connolly of No. 1 Commando went 'over the top' into a black night for reconnaissance. Selby stepped on a hidden mine and both were flung into the air. The Germans opened fire and the men crawled away in different directions, true to their training. Towards dawn, Connolly limped back to his unit but when the sun rose there was no sign of Selby. Three days elapsed before a sentry reported a figure crawling towards the lines. It was the lance corporal, blood-stained, emaciated and shivering in the wet and freezing conditions. Before being taken to hospital to have a badly fractured leg reset, Selby pin-pointed various German positions and strengths which, despite his pain, he had observed and noted during his sixty-hour ordeal.

The commando mission saved many thousands of Allied lives. The daring raids along the continental coasts forced the Germans to straggle their troops in a thin line from Norway right down to the Mediterranean. Mountbatten's commandos struck at one Norwegian island destroying installations and killing or capturing many Germans. It was the first raid in which all three services had combined, and it was so successful that for the rest of the war 400,000 of Hitler's crack troops were kept in Norway and thus out of harm's way. Other successes followed, notably the destruction of the special German radar station at Bruneval and the crippling of the vital dry dock at St Nazaire, both of which have been fully described many times on film and in books. One event which attracted neither Hollywood nor many writers was the raid on Dieppe. It scored no notable victory and proved extremely costly in lives. But it taught the Allies many lessons. Mountbatten was to say later, 'The successful landing in Normandy was won on the beaches of Dieppe.'

Dieppe did have its moments in the middle of the terrible slaughter. One of my fellow clansmen, Lord Fraser Lovat, and his commando unit stormed German pillboxes and eliminated many gun batteries. The Frasers, who originated in France and came over with William I, had through the centuries been fierce fighters and hard-dying men, and were now returning to attack an alien force ruling their country of origin. In one of the rare moments of calm on the Dieppe beaches, Fraser Lovat strolled calmly forth, like a laird walking on his Scottish estates, and, pulling out his hunting horn, rallied his men to charge another battery. With blood-curdling war cries he and his commandos swept aside the enemy leaving German bodies strewn in their wake. Pat Porteous, one of the commandos, sustained terrible wounds but continued to bayonet his way relentlessly through the battery. Afterwards he was awarded the Victoria Cross.

The experience gained in the Dieppe operation saved many thousands of lives and prevented the 'D' in D-Day standing for 'disaster'. Another incident that contributed to the success of our invasion also involved the commandos. Two months before D-Day, a pilot spotted an enemy boat hugging the Calais beaches and dived in for the kill. But his bombs had a strange effect – there were far too many plumes of water for the number of bombs that he had dropped. The amazed pilot and his crew had never seen anything like it before and, on landing, the debriefing officers were just as surprised. When the strange affair filtered up to the top, the commandos were called in to investigate. A unit of four experienced men was chosen from Combined Operations headquarters. The men, equipped with infra-red cameras, were ordered to investigate near Cap Griz Nez. (This location was quickly reached, allowing more time for detective work; and, if caught, the enemy might assume that the Cap would feature in the expected invasion.) The commando foursome solved the mystery within minutes of arriving. Hefty stakes had been driven into the sand, ready to pierce the hull of any landing craft. Attached to each stake was a high-explosive mine designed to explode after the stake had penetrated. The unit retired with samples and without being observed. Two months later a force of commandos preceded each landing craft to put out of action the enemy's nasty surprises.

Involved in this episode, as with many other previous missions, were the United States Rangers. In April 1942, General George Marshall, Roosevelt's Chief Military Adviser and Army Chief, heard of the commandos and Combined Operations and visited their operational headquarters. He was amazed at how Mountbatten had got the navy, army and airforce working as one unit, and speedily arranged for men from the American forces to visit the commando training centre at Achnacarry in Scotland.

Many a rookie's dreams were made or shattered on the bonny banks of Loch Arkaig, and today the nearby Commando Memorial draws back thousands each year, perhaps to recall the close camaraderie and toughness of those iron days. When the sun shines and the towering mountains admire their reflections in the nineteen-mile mirror of the still loch, it seems as though nothing has ever happened to mar this quiet Highland beauty spot. Yet, for the brave of yesteryear, the loch is haunted by the sounds of mock battle. Perhaps they again experience that awful silence while waiting to pounce. . . or be pounced upon. Even for those visiting for the first time there is an aura – one almost feels that the commandos are only away on some exercise, and will be back tomorrow. It is truly a moving memorial to those silent hidden heroes of yesterday.

Mountbatten, before his tragic death, wrote, 'Today, we are used to the daring exploits of James Bond 007, but the story of these gallant raiders – commandos and rangers – is even more exciting and gripping, for these were real men facing real-life danger.'

6

Odd orders!

The telephone rang. 'F-S?' It was my SOE contact. 'We need French cycling shoes this time.' The voice went on to give size, type and quality, and ended mysteriously:

'By the way, old boy, not new. The shoes must be well used but with plenty of life left in them.' The order was top priority and due out on the next drop over Normandy.

The call came as a welcome change at a time when office routine was becoming a little mundane. Even though I was supplying vital, life-saving gadgets day after day, whether they were tear-gas pens, false-bottom shaving brushes or special hollow golf balls, repetition made them bread-and-butter affairs. These odd telephone orders were a welcome and dramatic change to my diet. I was rarely told why the items were needed – not until much later. It was weeks, for instance, before I discovered the story that lay behind those cycling shoes.

Guillaume Mercader was a *Tour de France* cycling champion and the Germans liked winners, especially if at some future date the star might add to the prestige of the Third Reich. Sport made for great propaganda and Mercader was therefore given a special permit for his practice runs which virtually gave him the freedom of Normandy.

German troops and sentry guards would cheer him on his way — but his foremost achievement never entered their heads. D-Day was fast approaching and it was vital that every Resistance group in Normandy knew the exact moment when to strike. Mercader, actually an SOE worker, was entrusted with the names and addresses of every Resistance leader and given one of our miniature radios together with a secret sentence to listen for on BBC radio. At 6.30 pm on June 5th 1944, Mercader was stunned with excitement as he tuned in at the rear of his cycle shop in Bayeux.

'Madeleine!' he shouted to his wife, 'I'll be back late tonight.'

Mercader strapped on the second-hand cycling shoes which I had provided — new ones, impossible to get in France, might have made the ever-watchful Gestapo curious — and sped off into the summer evening on what looked like a normal training run. As he raced through Normandy he gave the Resistance leaders the codeword they had waited weeks to hear. The various Resistance groups knew exactly what to do next.

Albert Auge, a station master at Caen, and his Underground unit smashed the steam injectors on locomotives, destroyed water pumps and anything else to hinder the movement of German troops. André Farine, with his Resistance group at Lieu Fontaine, near Isigny, cut telephone cables, silencing Normandy's communications. Yves Gresselin, a Cherbourg grocer, and his team dynamited vital points on the railway network. One can imagine the havoc and confusion that took place. We had learned many lessons concerning the importance of clandestine resistance and disruption behind enemy lines since the unsupported frontal attack on Dieppe, when one in five was killed. On D-Day losses were reduced to one in sixty.

As dawn broke, and France's cycling Phidippides finished his marathon run, Hitler's Atlantic Wall of defence around the Normandy coast began to crumble. British warships and 9,000 bombers struck pre-selected targets with incredible accuracy. This, odd as it may sound, was partly due to the French-textured wool I had provided for one of our women agents. She was a bona fide farmer's wife and travelled miles in crammed buses, knitting needles clicking rapidly, pausing occasionally to make notes on her pattern book.

'Knit one, purl two, gun battery three,' was her mental arithemetic as she wove Normandy's defences into her work. After her travels, she would hand her pattern book to the Chief of Resistance in her area. The positions of new defences, roads and troop strengths together with their equipment and locations collected by her and other agents were then collated and sent on to London.

One of the most urgent orders I ever received seemed one of the most puzzling. I was asked to supply ninety miles of red tape! No reason was given. As I telephoned my various contacts to fulfil the order, I could not help smiling. Red tape was one of the wartime horrors that I had so far avoided. When the Treasury, against my advice, once insisted on a costing officer accompanying me to one of my firms to investigate an invoice which they considered too high, I found that the director had charged only the cost of manufacture and left off his own profit margin. I tore up the invoice and told the director to hand the costing officer a new invoice with the wartime legitimate profit added. The Treasury never again bothered me with this type of red tape!

My paper work was kept to an absolute minimum. The names and addresses of my 300 suppliers, including many famous commercial companies, were kept in an ordinary HMSO (indexed) pocket book, which I still have in my personal museum. All contact and ordering was done either face-to-face or over the telephone. Secrecy and correspondence files had always seemed to be contradictory partners and I ensured that no 'tapery' enmeshed my office. I occasionally risked reprimand and even the sack from my Ministry of Supply superiors, who never knew the full range of my activities. I always felt fairly safe, as MI6 would have bailed me out. I was designated an ordinary temporary civil servant in Clothing and Textiles (CT) for the armed forces. When my staff and I moved in, three clothing and textile sections were already in existence, all sedately and neatly wrapped in red tape. There was CT1, handling clothes for the Navy, CT2 for the Army and CT3 for the Air Force. I was CT6. The other CT directors would occasionally frown at me as I entered their offices which resembled Wall Street during a ticker-tape welcome. They knew that I supplied MI9 with prisoner of war supplies because of the sample packages which regularly arrived from my contacts. They dubbed my CT department 'Comforts for Troops', which I found a conveniently innocent front. They might have adopted my own private insignia of 'Charles's Tricks', except that all secret gadgets and equipment went directly to an outside depot from where they were redistributed to MI6, MI9, SOE and, later in the war, to the Special Air

Service (SAS). Even the Director of Clothing and Textiles, G. Ritchie Rice, who officially was my boss, was unaware of the real nature of my work. He was flabbergasted when he read my first book, *The Secret War of Charles Fraser-Smith*[1]. He would have been appalled at the lack of office formalities had he known, and yet it was this total lack of red tape that brought in the high-priority order for ninety miles of it. True to form, we delivered the goods within hours.

After the flap, came the facts. 'Sealion', the code name for the German invasion of England, was under way and, as a consequence, so too was a top priority operation of our own, code named 'Fish'. Hitler might invade and take our land but certainly not our wealth. Dozens of our fastest merchant and naval ships were commandeered to float our gold and bank securities across the Atlantic. The whole operation was carried out under a cover of incredible secrecy, for a leak might have started a run on principal banks – or even worse. A school of German submarines might have arranged a mid-ocean feast at our expense. The 'Fish' ships took only a few tons on any one trip and, amazingly, not one ingot was lost. The tons of securities also arrived safely – tied up with the ninety miles of red tape I had supplied. Once across the Atlantic, the securities were safely entombed in the large granite building of the Sun Life Assurance Company in Montreal's Dominion Square. It had deep underground warrens reaching forty-five feet below street level, and the only access was by one elevator with the final entrance secured by a double-combination lock. The transfer of securities, after arriving in Montreal by train, was always

1. Published in Great Britain by Michael Joseph Ltd.

completed at night. The following morning, the Sun Life staff arrived for another routine day, unaware of one of the greatest-ever hoards of riches below their feet.

One official in the 'know' was dining in the Sun Life restaurant shortly after the last of the securities had arrived.

'Isn't the news awful!' said his worried waitress. 'If the Germans land in Southampton, I hope they don't take the shares I have there.' The official would dearly have loved to have reassured her that her shares were only a few dozen feet below where he was sitting.

In June 1940 I was still in Morocco, where I had worked for fourteen years as a Christian missionary looking after orphanages and also the farms of the Moroccan royal family. On June 10th I tuned into Turkish radio, which was generally an hour or two ahead of British and French broadcasts, and heard the following:

'Turkey calling. Turkey calling. Italy declares war against Britain and France.'

This began my active involvement in World War II. I immediately telephoned the French Government HQ in Morocco, who denied any knowledge of Italy's entrance into the war.

'Ring Paris, and have it confirmed,' I suggested. The Moroccan French government apparently believed me. Within minutes an official rang back thanking me for my prompt warning. Four days later Paris was captured by German forces.

Retired French officer, Commandant Hugot, and other colonists approached me the following day. They did not trust General Nogués, the French Governor General of Morocco, and they wanted to fight and resist from North Africa. On ringing the British Consul General at Rabat I was curtly told that there were no orders from England concerning resistance. I asked if I should get to England and help from there. Again the Consul General said that he had no instructions, and told me to stay put. This seemed anything but satisfactory. Going down to Rabat, on the coast, an Arab friend told me that the Consul General had sent his family to America! Realizing that he was a total let-down, I immediately went to Casablanca where I discovered that English shipping directors and agents had slipped away to America or South Africa. If I remained much longer I would probably spend the rest of the war interned or doing little but produce food for Vichy France and the Germans. I thought my war effort should be channelled in other directions, and was fortunate to find a Norwegian boat, loaded with phosphates, waiting to leave for England. The captain agreed to take me and I telephoned my wife and small son to come and join me.

Meanwhile, I popped in to see the British Consul in Casablanca but found him engaged on the phone. Waiting outside the door of his office, I overheard him phoning the French Governor General and stating that Britain would deliver aeroplanes and war material to Casablanca if he would lead resistance. The French Governor General had other ambitions in line with his pro-Fascist leanings, and refused. What a difference it would have made to the war if our ships supplying Malta and Egypt had had this air cover in the Mediterranean! As it was, more than eighty per cent of them were lost or damaged and the long route around the Cape delayed urgently needed supplies.

I returned to collect my family and boarded the

SS *Varenberg* and waited for clearance to sail. Twice it came through only to be rescinded at the last minute. The interminable waiting was relieved by the arrival of an impressive convoy of French, Polish and Belgian ships, including the pride of the French navy, the *Jean Bart*. Five French boats carried 1,500 tons of gold, and they too were anxious to avoid the enemy. This convoy had been in the French ports of Brest and Lorient three days after Paris fell. They were to have sailed for America but were hurriedly dispatched to sea only a few hours before advance German units arrived. Five days later France surrendered to Germany and the gold convoy received orders to go to Casablanca. Within hours of arriving, the convoy was again under way — this time bound for Dakar, the main port of the French West African possession of Senegal. A little later, we too slipped anchor and raced out of harbour as fast as our cargo of phosphates would allow. We eventually arrived safely in England where I took up my secret work in London.

Dakar was considered to be of strategic importance and Britain reckoned that it might be used by the Germans as a submarine base in the battle of the Atlantic. The gold was also needed to finance the Free French cause, as well as Polish and Belgian resistance, and it was decided, in collusion with de Gaulle, to land Free French forces and take over the port. Unfortunately, some of the Free French officers could not contain their enthusiasm at returning to a French possession. In a restaurant in Liverpool where the assault force was being assembled, the officers raised their glasses to 'Dakar!'. The incident filtered through to Vichy France, and Marshal Pétain immediately ordered a large naval force and pro-Vichy regiments to the Senegal city.

When our intelligence service informed Churchill of what had happened, he was in favour of calling off the operation, but de Gaulle insisted that it should go ahead. The outcome was a humiliating failure with deplorable mistakes and results. For instance, de Gaulle sent his envoys into Dakar to negotiate before attacking, and one of his officials carried a list of Frenchmen dedicated to the Free French cause. He was relieved of the list, which was later put to treacherous use. It was from this point onwards that we felt we could not trust de Gaulle's wisdom, nor that of his entourage. His actions often proved a liability to Britain and America in the war, and unfortunately, his attitude to us afterwards was at times quite venomous.

When it was clear that Dakar would not allow the Allies to land and that British battleships could force it into subjection only by means of a long siege and probable severe loss of life, Churchill called the enterprise off.

The gold was finally immobilized for the rest of the war, together with twenty French ships and their thousands of trained sailors, in the French West Indies. Also impounded were 110 American aircraft which had been sent to France to help her in her hour of need. These planes had been diverted to Casablanca when France collapsed, in the hope that French forces in Morocco and Algeria would continue the war, together with the British, from North Africa. I saw these crated planes in Casablanca before sailing on our Norwegian boat.

At the end of the war France's immobilized gold was recovered intact, and provided the basis for rebuilding the French economy. Those in Britain who looked askance at France's good fortune (with some reason, it must be admitted), had even more grounds for complaint with regard to their own country's postwar problems. The British gold which had been evacuated was largely expended in payment to the United States under the terms of the 'Cash and Carry' scheme. My sympathies lie with those who saw this scheme as ruinously unfair. Britain had to pay a crippling price for the defence of the Free World – a stupendous £3,600,000,000. It was a major contributing factor to our postwar economic crises and undoubtedly lies behind many of our contemporary financial troubles.

It was only after I had been with CT6 – MI6 for a few weeks that I discovered why Turkish radio was always the first with the news, especially war announcements. I learned that many MI6 agents were in Istanbul in a bid to win the war of espionage. I found that it was my job to provide the material to help them – jewellery. All combatant countries of World War II had their top secret agents stationed in the Turkish capital, passing to each other misinformation, juicy titbits and a little genuine news to lend credence to their leaks. This was done in the hope of bartering information from their opposite numbers. When shopping in this international spy market, agents found it useful to have a few inducements. They were expecially interested in syphoning information out of, or through, the city's sloe-eyed beauties who might have liaisons with the enemy. I had one of my London firms run me up a quantity of necklaces and bracelets for this purpose, costing up to £10,000 each. In those days that was a fortune but well worth it if the information gleaned, or the misinformation passed on, saved Allied lives.

There was one particularly amusing incident, which had a happy ending. We had delegated a Scot to befriend a beautiful and intelligent Austrian woman in the hope that the gift of a large gold and sapphire broach (supplied by me) would win her allegiance. But a German secret agent quickly stepped in and took first place in her affections. Later, an American agent swept her off with an even more glittering present. The young woman eventually discovered that her three suitors were all agents and as bitterly opposed to Hitler as she in fact was. Even the German found her preferable to his Führer and eventually defected to the Americans. The foursome then formed themselves into a combined operations alliance and proved themselves a formidable force, much to our delight.

7

Those who dared

The commander crouched on the hillside and waited for dawn to unveil the enemy. In a few hours they would be his executioners, unless a miracle happened. The Middle East sun peeked above the opposite range and it was as though a giant, invisible brush painted golden contours across what had been a black nothingness. The brush seemed to run dry in one vast area leaving a dark streak across the valley floor. The commander's imagination, kindled by the stress of the coming battle, pictured the enemy encampment as a swarm of locusts. He imagined their military equipment and transport to be as numerous as the grains of sand in the desert itself. The sun had climbed high before the commander's scouts returned with reports which, though less fanciful, were still as terrifying. The enemy tally was 135,000 troops, outnumbering his own men four hundred and fifty to one! Tonight, he would be told to attack!

The commander had, in the past, viewed his immediate superior with respectful awe. The military strategy of previous encounters had been impeccable and above reproach. But this time. . .?

The situation might have been acceptable had the General left him with his original command of 32,000 even though the odds would still have been over four to one against. But to select just 300 –

the cream though they were – and withdrew the remainder from the battle zone altogether, appeared to be a premeditated exercise in suicide. To add to the frustration and fear, the weaponry requisitioned to them was not so much laughable as verging on the hysterical. Their arsenal consisted of a few dozen torches, earthenware jars and, of all things, the instruments of the regimental brass band! The General had suggested that the 300 men be divided into three groups and positioned so as to encircle the enemy. Each man was to be armed with a trumpet and a jar in which was to be hidden a lighted torch. At a signal, the men were to smash open the jars, wave their flaring torches in the night and blow their trumpets furiously. They were then to advance, shouting 'A sword for God and Gideon'.

Those who know their Bible will appreciate that my department can claim no credit for supplying this particular outfit! Gideon and his Divine General needed no help from MI6/CT6 as their suprise night attack caused the Midianites to panic and slaughter each other leaving the remnant to retreat in a demoralized rabble. But CT6 was very much involved in the World War II equivalent of Gideon's force.

Many of our top military men, with their biblical upbringing, realized the fascinating potential of small mobile groups to create havoc among the armies of orthodoxy. Ord Wingate's Burma Chindits were actually modelled on the Gideon strategy. Field Marshal Montgomery's use of small units was also an ingredient in his success. It was this thinking which brought about the birth of Britain's shock and speed squads which were to become known as the Special Air Service (SAS).

One SAS operation was virtually a replay of the Gideon affair.

The leader of the SAS unit surveyed the enemy air base, noting that as usual his mini-squad was outnumbered hundreds to one. A large German detachment stood guard along one side of the runway tending the parked planes. An Italian force mirrored their activities opposite them. Under the cover of darkness, the SAS squad moved in, working silently and unseen. In the early hours dawn exploded prematurely as dozens of flares and charges were triggered off. In the ensuing confusion, the two sets of defenders opened fire on each other, sheltering behind the strewn wreckage of burning planes. The raid was devastatingly successful, crippling many planes and causing havoc among the enemy.

In command of that raid was Lieutenant David Stirling, the man whose efforts were largely responsible for bringing the SAS into being. His involvement with small groups began in 1940 as a member of the Special Unit led by Robert Laycock. The 'Lay Force', as it was nicknamed, had much opposition and little success and the top brass were delighted to disband it after only a few months. But David Stirling, a tenacious Scotsman, had seen a potential which petty jealousies and politics had killed off before it could be realized. Stirling's ability and strength of mind were as formidable as his physical stature (nearly two metres), and he set about making his own plans.

When his small group blueprint was completed, the problem remained of how to bypass the pigeon holes of jealousy which had proved Laycock's downfall. Stirling, despite his lowly rank, decided to reach for the general's stars and marched into command headquarters. The guard was easily tricked and the lieutenant boldly stepped into the deputy commander's office, fired a quick apology and launched into his well-rehearsed sales pitch. Before General Ritchie could squeeze in a protest, his curiosity was engaged. Stirling shifted up a gear into a confident flow until Ritchie registered profound interest and promised to submit the plans to the C-in-C, General Auchinleck. The war situation in North Africa at that time could not have been worse. Churchill was demanding results and 'The Auk' was ready to try any feasible plan. Stirling was given the go-ahead.

The lieutenant forcast a 'Sterling victory' but his first efforts fell as flat as his pun. He decided that parachuting would be the best means of reaching his targets, but no instructor could be located. To a human dynamo like Stirling, this was an insignificant detail. He quickly arranged for a friend to take him aloft in an old Valencia, and out he jumped. A split second later he was whirling in a sky-diver's nightmare with his canopy caught on the tail plane. He eventually plunged earthward, torn silk streaming like a Roman Candle above his head. He sustained leg and back injuries which put him in Alexandria Hospital. There he seethed in his immobility. It did, however, give him valuable time to think of ways to outwit his opponents in the lower ranks of high command. He found for instance that the adjutant-general's department for supplies in Egypt, known as Q, presented insurmountable difficulties, and he was told that he would have to 'queue at Q' and wait months before getting anything. This poor joke did not amuse Stirling. Not only did he set about acquiring tents and equipment out there by unorthodox means, but my Q department was able to come to his help.

My 1940-45 notebook gives details of special daggers, German and other uniforms, Arab clothing, desert sand-goggles and secret gadgets, a few of which are still on the classified list. German uniforms were always in demand, and I had even been commissioned to have a copy made of Hess's uniform shortly after his flight to Scotland. We were able to duplicate it right down to the correct weave and fibre.

Parachuting was again to bring Stirling near to failure, this time on his first official operation. High winds scattered his men and equipment like fluffy dandelion-clock seeds, and they wasted valuable time searching for each other and regrouping. Timing, for which I had provided the very best watches, was all important in these small-group raids, and Stirling eventualy decided that parachuting was about as reliable as a white ball bobbing round a roulette wheel. He threw in his lot with the already established and successful Long Range Desert Group, who had the sands and their treachery mapped and memorized from months of reconnaissance. Stirling's men were mainly explosives experts and fierce fighters, and the two groups combined neatly. One delivered: the other demolished.

The desert was ideal for this purpose. Along the Mediterranean coast was the only road, stretching hundreds of miles; on each side were the supply dumps, petrol stores, camps, repair depots and airfields of the enemy. Inland was a vast expanse of desert impossible to control. Small trained groups could move there at night unseen, and lie hidden during the day. Their trucks would be draped with camouflage nets supplied by our Ministry of Supply Department, and from the air their small encampments were impossible to distinguish from the patches of surrounding scrub, or sand hillocks. Under the cover of darkness they would silently place their time-bombs, and vanish back into their camouflaged lairs. When missions were completed they returned to their own lines.

David Stirling's operations were recognized to be highly economical in casualties and material, producing surprise and success. But despite this, General Headquarters again and again failed to exploit the colossal potential SAS offered as a new and vital weapon of modern warfare.

The obstructionists continued to be a nagging irritant, and Stirling was often forced to take the law into his own hands to prove the value of his units. One night one of his squads staggered the critics at General Headquarters by destroying nearly 100 German planes on the ground. Later aerial photography revealed a devastated scrapyard where once had been one of Germany's most threatening desert airfields. Raids similar to this caused the enemy to double and then redouble their sentries, and on most airfields each plane was given a round-the-clock guard diverting thousands of troops away from the fighting zones. The Germans had 900 operational planes in North Africa. Stirling's men were responsible for destroying or crippling nearly half of them. Each operation took a handful of men and a few pounds of explosives. It proved the best value for money in World War II, and it gave Rommel his most persistent headache. Dozens of night raids forced the German Field Marshal to move his men and supplies by day, and the RAF bombers were then only too happy to use them for target practice. No wonder Field-Marshal Rommel wrote in his diary, 'Lieutenant-Colonel David Stirling's SAS caused us more damage than any other British unit of equal strength.'

A daring episode particularly distressed Rommel. One evening French prisoners of war were escorted by German guards into his most impregnable North African airfield. In the early hours of the following morning the prisoners and their guards were found to have vanished, and so too had the planes, hangers, military installations and officers. All that was left was a smoking rubble. I well remember supplying our men with German and French uniforms for that particular raid.

It was extraordinary that the enemy did not send out patrols to follow Stirling's groups and seek to capture them. They tried to track them by reconnaissance planes and obliterate them by bombing and strafing.

It seemed that the Italians and Germans disliked the empty desert. The British, coming from a seafaring people used to navigating vast open spaces, were more at home in the uncharted sands. The sea and the desert have much in common.

Our desert groups were equipped by my department with theodolites and prismatic compasses. Water was a priority, and I supplied special filters and chemicals to help purify any water found, however brackish. In dire necessity they had tablets to enable them to drink their own urine.

Men like Stirling, together with others – C.E. (Dare) Newell, Majors Carr and Elder and Lieutenant Forsythe - with whom I had regular supply contacts proved that small forces can play a decisive role in overturning a massive enemy. Often, they were more effective than a frontal attack by a couple of divisions. The slow-moving regular war machine, with its formidable mass of guns and armour-plating, could offer little defence against the shock and speed of small groups like the SAS or Combined Operations Commandos.

General Auckinleck was so impressed with the outworking of Stirling's plans that he obtained approval for the SAS to have its own badge and insignia - a winged dagger with the motto, 'Who dares wins'. Stirling was promoted to major.

The man who dares, who retains his individualism, is ready for isolated initiative in any emergency. The man who can act unsupervised and yet allows himself to be part of a team cannot be equalled. This was proved time and again in the Falklands crisis and also in the Iranian Embassy siege in 1980, when it took the SAS a matter of seconds to eliminate terrorists and free the hostages. The principles and tactics which were first tried out so successfully in those desert days of North Africa were acted out to perfection equally in the near-arctic South Atlantic and on the streets and rooftops of London. Before attacking two facts are always determined - the number of the enemy and the pattern of their movements. The modern SAS, of course, have much more sophisticated equipment than I could provide in the forties. Their latest surveillance systems can pick up every word and disagreement among the enemy, whether they be terrorists or illegal invaders. By doing this they determine the exact psychological moment of weakness before striking.

The vast majority of expert commentators on the Falklands Campaign agreed that the success of the many small SAS intelligence-gathering patrols was a major factor in the ultimate victory. Major-General Edward Furzdon, Defence Correspondent of the Daily Telegraph, said:

> They operated both in the offensive mode - to provoke the Argentines to give away information - and in the passive one of reporting from close proximity observation.

> The dedication, daring, cheek, and professional skill they applied to this part of their varied spectrum of activities reflected well the demanding standards of their specialist training, their flexibility in adapting to a very different environment and their experience gained from Northern Ireland and elsewhere.

> One very important lesson of the outcome is to appreciate the sheer quantity of detailed intelligence such highly-trained well-positioned teams can generate.

There is no doubt that against today's terrorists or the intricate bureaucracy of massed armed forces the small and flexible team is indispensable. It has been reassuring to learn from recent military action that such teams are still available – but for how long?

With each new decade, the voices of opposition climb a few more decibels urging that we surrender to some dream of neutrality. Our society increasingly equates spending on armament and defence with madness. But we forget too readily; our memory blurs over Hungary, Afghanistan, Poland, and the annexation of parts of the Third World. We tolerate communism. Often we fail to appreciate the Soviet Union's true aim: territorial domination. Today's Kremlin is in the same business as was the Third Reich in the thirties.

World War II was basically a struggle for freedom. In Hitler's masterplan, Britain - and eventually the rest of the world - was to be forcibly enrolled into one vast slave camp. The residents of Germany were themselves little more than servants. Manfred Rommel, son of the famous Field Marshal, closes his foreword to Allan Tute's book, *The North Africa War,* with the following:

> In a short time, enemies have become friends and allies, and we have to thank the honourable attitude of the Western Allies towards a defeated Germany for making this possible. But it is also the determination of Germany never again to surrender her reclaimed democracy to a dictatorship.

Dictators live on in all parts of our shrinking globe. Most have moderate ambitions but the Russian version wishes to enslave the world, just as it has done its own people. Freedom of expression is allowed only if you happen to be a convinced Marxist. There is no liberty of movement unless you have your own private tunnel under the Iron Curtain. There is no freedom of religion unless your god is spelt 's-t-a-t-e'.

Against this, western society appears to have only one line of defence — a severe 'Tut-tut'. It attempts to mobilize a fickle world opinion that always degenerates into old-fashioned appeasement – rechristened 'détente'. Our pseudo-Christian culture wallows in a sentimental trough of tolerance, love and peace, forgetting that human nature has not improved noticably since Cain murdered Abel, and certainly not since Hitler. Idealists believe that mankind is evolving, *en route* to perfection, though the evidence points in the opposite direction. We still murder, rape, thieve and lust after power. The evil in human nature that engineered World War II is still with us today, and we go on yearning for the outer trappings of life and superficial material satisfaction.

Prince Charles, talking to London's Press Club, saw the problem in religious terms. About our liberty he said:

> We are free to choose whether we remain aware of our inner selves or concentrate purely on our outer, in which case we increase the danger of being overcome by what one can only describe as evil. Our protection depends, I believe, on the mystical power which, from time immemorial, has been called God and whose relationship to man seems to depend on man's relationship to his inner voice.

God himself sums up what is the only common-sense course open to our nation today. Through his Son he says: 'When a strong man, fully armed, guards his possessions he is safe and lives in peace.'

Our country did not think much of that advice in the thirties. Consequently, we brought upon ourselves and the world a terrifying agony. In five years tens of millions were murdered, wounded, or made homeless refugees.

'Butter before tanks. . . Peace at any price. . . ' The voices of appeasement were heard, even as German Panzer divisions went through Europe as a knife travels through butter.

Within a decade of the war being over, Britain again wanted welfare before weapons; this crescendoed into the eighties. Then came the Falkland crisis; and once again we began to realize the importance of being strong and fully armed. Had President Galtieri postponed his invasion for a decade we might not have had the resources to respond!

Whether or not we retain and build on what we have depends on who wins the national ear and who controls the national purse. There will be other tinpot dictators to deal with in the future, even without taking into consideration the menace of Russia.

Just as we allowed Nazism and Facism to arm and spread in the thirties, so we are now allowing the same facility to Communism. Two-thirds of the world's population know little of democracy, and if Britain and the free West wish to retain a working knowledge of the same, then we need to have the resources to protect ourselves. We need an efficient Secret Service. Our armed forces need to be strong, capable and adequately equipped. Our deterrents, nuclear or otherwise, cost billions; but it is a small price to pay for liberty and peace, and to avert the wastage of millions of lives.

The French Maquis, another of my wartime customers, knew well the horrors of seeing their country ruled by dictatorial foreigners. May Britain never have the same need to exhibit such courage.

8

The unconquered

French agents on the Gestapo payroll outnumbered the Germans by as many as twenty to one. In the city of Marseilles alone, a thousand French spies were under the control of fifty Germans. It was the same ratio in Saint-Etienne, Loire, where captured records showed fifteen Germans directing the fifth column network of 300. The Milice, a French Gestapo force, headed by Joseph Darnaud, a brothel owner of Nice, numbered more than 200,000. Ten thousand francs were paid for each person denounced, plus generous expenses.

We ended the war wondering by what kind of miracle the work of SOE and that of the French Resistance and Maquis had managed to survive against such odds. They had also to run the unseen gauntlet of part-time collaborators – thousands of Frenchmen who sold their neighbours and loved ones for power, greed or merely to keep on the safe side of the ubiquitous SS.

Rich landowner Philippe de Vomecourt fell comfortably into this last category, according to the Gestapo files covering his home town of Souesmes in Northern France. An index card detailed his collaboration. He had frequently entertained officers of all ranks, taking them game-shooting on his well-stocked estate. Other hospitality had been provided to boost officer morale. He had also reported sighting British planes circling over his land together with his suspicion that paratroopers had landed. Half-buried canopies had later been found in the estate's woods. Many similar entries confirmed to the Gestapo that de Vomecourt was an amiable and co-operative friend of the Fatherland and could be trusted as a gentleman of good breeding. The index card was soon transformed into a weighty file of favourable acts, and the landowner continued to enjoy German patronage and the consequent freedom and security it gave to him. He enjoyed rather less the displeasure and coolness of certain neighbours whose sympathies lay on the opposite side of the Channel.

It was not until late 1944 that the Gestapo and the derisive locals began to see de Vomecourt in a fresh light. As a result of certain incidents, his large file was transferred to a new home. It was evicted from the ranks of collaborators and relocated at the top of the 'most wanted' list at SS Headquarters. Before the Germans finally retreated, the file boasted a 2,000,000 franc bounty on the dead-or-alive head of its subject.

Philippe de Vomecourt was, in fact, 'our man in Souesmes'. He and most of his Maquisards outwitted and outlived their oppressors and were a heroic example of how small flexible groups can confound thousands of the enemy, keeping them safely away from the front line and the Allies. Philippe had fled to England when France collapsed. His first stop was London's Free French headquarters where, despite continuous pleas, General de Gaulle rejected his plans for active resistance. The French landowner eventually contacted our Special Operations Executive and was speedily posted to one of its first primitive training schools in Scotland. De Vomecourt celebrated his graduation by parachuting onto his French doorstep with the best equipment that I could provide. His mission: to establish friendly links with the Germans while setting up and training a small group of Maquis.

Both these tasks were to prove easier than might be imagined. The Germans were quite gullible when it came to enjoying the high life and home comforts, and de Vomecourt's luxury amenities were welcomed without too many questions. The enemy also assisted unintentially with his undercover recruitment. Their policy of 'forced labour' in factories sent many young and competent Frenchmen fleeing to the hills with no other choice but to sign up for the Maquis or other Resistance groups.

Back in London, we busied ourselves assembling the tools that de Vomecourt would need for the second part of his work. Explosives and arms of every variety were packed into parachute containers which I had had designed especially for this purpose. Only one problem eventually remained: how to deliver the equipment without arousing suspicion. It was de Vomecourt who came up with a simple but highly satisfactory solution. The drop went ahead. He and his first Maquis recruits collected and hid the containers in a forest of rhododendrons on the estate and then planted, as decoys, partly destroyed and buried parachutes, the ones which eventually found their way into de Vomecourt's SS file. He deserved an Oscar nomination for his bluff. The search troops, on finding the canopies, followed freshly made footprints to a nearby stream, and then jumped to the conclusion already prepared for them. Enemy agents or paratroopers had obviously made off along the stream, one way or another, and then left it at a suitable bridge or road, leaving no trace on the hard surface. The searchers, having thanked their informant for his co-operation, departed to begin an area-wide search involving hundreds more soldiers. This left Philippe's fledgling Maquis unit to start its training in peace. And that is the way it remained except for the occasional rest days when the German officers came for a shoot.

Philippe next established an SOE-supplied radio operator in a nearby garage, the one the Germans used for their repairs. Garage owner Antoine Vincent adopted the habit of saving his noisiest jobs for transmission times. Once regular radio contact was established, we were able to begin an intensive delivery of arms, equipment, food and money at interchangeable dropping zones in the surrounding hills as part of the long build up to D-Day.

This was just one of many similarly armed and trained Maquis units of French patriots, the unconquered who lived concealed in the brushwood undergrowth of the hilly, desolate regions of France. *Maquis* is actually the Corsican word for 'brushwood'. The groups had only the barest of essentials, drew no pay and lived in the wilds, surviving on short rations. I was able to have supplies of food and French Menier chocolate (made in London) dropped to them from time to time.

The Maquis should not be confused with the French Resistance. They left family, friends and home for their brushwood existence, while the Resistance worked mainly from home. A Resistance worker, for instance, might be a legitimate labourer on Hitler's Atlantic Wall who could, with careful carelessness, mix the wrong aggregate of sand and cement. The Maquis fighter was more likely to emerge from nowhere to blow a breach in the wall with a well-placed ball of plastic explosive.

The Maquis organized themselves in an extensive range of guerilla activities. Their objective was to tie down as many enemy divisions as possible with hit-and-run raids, sabotaging communications and transport to create general disruption and a spirit of defeatism. This nerve-wracking subversive warfare included the blowing up of installations and, in quieter moments of the war, polishing their skills by demolishing culverts or dropping a row of trees across a major trunk road. The ultimate objective was to train men who, when the invasion started, would be equipped to attack and disrupt enemy communications in order to make life and progress easier for our men on the Normandy beach-heads.

One of Philippe de Vomecourt's coups was the magnificent operation at the German Michenon Camp. This was an armaments depot of immense importance, exceptionally well-guarded and surrounded by an impenetrable electrified system. Philippe arranged by radio for the RAF to bomb it on D-Day − 1, and while this was in progress, it was reasonably easy for him and his fifty Maquisards to blow up the surrounding railway lines and roads. The immobilization of vital war material was a serious blow to the Germans, but a matter of life and death for the advancing Allies. The Germans felt unable to admire de Vomecourt's daring, nor did they appreciate more than 200 of their guards being killed or wounded during the Michenon raid. A frustrated high command set their network of French spies and collaborators the priority of locating this rebel unit – with some success. 400 SS troops were despatched to liquidate the Maquisards who had been spotted in the woods near

Souesmes. Philippe fortunately had his own informants and his underground band fled, but only to a more strategic position in the hills. There, in more favourable terrain, they turned to face the oncoming Germans. Hit-and-run skirmishes flared up during many hours and finally 214 exhausted Germans retreated leaving the remainder of their force dead or wounded. The Maquis lost just nine men, all of whom had been cornered and had either fought to the death or killed themselves. Death was always preferable to capture and the inevitable torture to death, and the possibility of giving something to the enemy.

The Allies were soon sweeping inland and the Maquis continued to harass and molest the overstretched and under-equipped Germans. In early September, 1944, de Vomecourt, now with 2,000 Maquisards under his command, started to hem in a demoralized force of 18,000 Germans under General Elster. The General was responsible for many atrocities in Northern France, and fearing reprisals from the French, he hastily retired to surrender to an advancing American division. The Americans treated him leniently, and the locals, who had had everything stolen from them and their kindred mutilated and murdered, have to this day never forgiven them for their softness.

De Vomecourt and his men had many narrow escapes but survived the war safely. Not all were as fortunate. Not all of the groups had the meticulous and audacious leadership which took the minimum of risks with the utmost security. In less disciplined groups, members were a little too informal and careless. Many Frenchmen were much too keen to let their friends and relatives know of their bravado. One Maquis group at Vercors, for instance, made a tragic mistake which stemmed from over-confidence. They went in for a pitched battle with the SS shortly after the Allies landed in the South of France. They were all but wiped out. Iron discipline and hit-and-run were the two golden rules of long life and success in the underground. They may not have sparkled with romance and courage, but they were the most effective.

Records show that those Maquis groups who were well-armed and thought they could fight the Germans in a battle were sooner or later surrounded and slaughtered, while those who used hit-and-run tactics to the full were the ones who did the maximum damage with the minimum losses.

We dropped arms for some 150,000 Maquisards, and thousands more armed themselves with weapons taken or stolen from German troops and arsenals, or from the Milice.

Pierre Rayon on Mount Ventoux practised the golden rules to perfection. He allowed an SS contingent, sent to wipe his group out, to advance in its tanks and lorries well into their mountain stronghold. This was permitted without a shot being fired or a Maquisard being seen. The Germans eventually found that they could go no further with their vehicles and began to turn round. It was then, from behind rocks and camouflaged hide-outs, that a merciless rain of bullets struck them. Explosions echoed around the mountains as Maquisards blew up the road to prevent stray tanks escaping. It was decimation for the SS as they retreated on foot. Even then Rayon held back. To attack would have meant a shoot-out and possible loss of men. Instead, he sent men ahead to hide behind rocks and to pick off the Germans as they retreated. 250 of the enemy were killed and Rayon did not lose a single man.

Successful Maquis or Resistance groups never allowed themselves to be encumbered with anything beyond the bare essentials, enabling them to strike or vanish at will.

In the first hours of our invasion of France, Maquis and Resistance groups, all supplied by SOE, mounted hundreds of raids at key rail junctions and military installations. It caused chaos for eight German divisions who were stranded miles from the front line. The saboteurs maintained rail stoppages at an even greater rate than the massive combined Allied air forces were able to do. One SS division, equipped with the latest German tanks, was ordered from Toulouse to Normandy on D-Day 1. The Maquis and Resistance forces turned the normal seventy-two hour journey into a nightmare obstacle course so that it was nearly three weeks before the Germans could join the fight. Had this first-class German division arrived earlier, it would have caused colossal havoc to a bridgehead that was already badly affected by the weather and other handicaps.

Resistance workers were able to cut nearly all the main telephone cables which forced the enemy to use radio – a great advantage to the Allies because we had broken their codes.

Awkward questions have been asked about the Resistance organized by our SOE. Was it really worthwhile? One of the main critics was Air Marshal Harris, who dismissed the effort as being next to useless. He refused to help with planes, considering that more damage could be done from the air. However, Bomber Command often lost in one night more men than the SOE lost in the entire war. SOE damage was also far more potent than Harris's thousand-bomber raids. Small explosive charges placed in the right position did far more damage to production than a long night of bombs, and at a fraction of the cost to French life and materials. SOE's unnerving and extensive operations also broke the German will to fight infinitely more than did massive bombing which tended to stiffen their will, as did the enemy bombing of England in 1940-1 bolster our resolve.

Criticisms about organization were, however, much nearer the mark. The SOE and the Resistance could not stand comparison to MI6, which has always been a permanent and highly organized section. SOE and the Resistance in France had not only teething troubles and certain elements in Britain against them, but a large number of Franco-German collaborationists. These were far more dangerous than the Germans. The French Government (Pétain and Vichy) were also strongly hostile to the Resistance. When the Vatican accepted the legality of the Vichy Government, it posed yet another dilema to the Resistance fighters, many of whom were ardent Roman Catholics. Many Jewish refugees who joined the Resistance also had their troubles. Marshal Pétain and the Vichy Government approached the Vatican concerning anti-semitic legislation, and the Pope said that he had no objection to it. Originally, an anti-semitic policy was foisted on the French but in the end Vichy went beyond the German demands. The Vichy round-up of the Jews was planned with military precision. 9,000 French police and 400 young French Fascists in uniform arrested 12,884 Jews on July 17th, 1942. Fewer than 400 survived the privations and camps.

The Resistance also had a subtle foe in the form of French authors and newspaper owners who kept their names alive by lending their pens and brains to the German cause. The French Communist Resistance groups were not very co-operative either. They were under the control of Moscow, and even when Russia became our ally, they still refused to unite with other groups. Their main aim was political and they intended to get control of France under Moscow when the war ended.

Possibly one of the most effective groups to help after D-Day were the *cheminots* – the rail workers. They were able to provide day-to-day information of all German rail transport of materials and men. By collecting this intelligence, we could then tell them which trains to delay or even derail. There were so many miles of track that it was impossible for the Germans to patrol most of it.

Rail sabotage of one sort and another became known as the *Bataille du Rail*. On D-Day, two-thirds of the railway system in the Normandy area was rendered useless to the German forces. Infinitely more damage was done to the railways by the Resistance than by Allied bombing and with far less danger to French workers and citizens. In one area, 180 German trains were derailed and 500 lines cut with no loss of life to the French. On D-Day + 1 the resistance in Burgundy prevented all trains running. Every method was used. For instance, a German troop train ran out of fuel having only completed a part of the journey. The German officer in charge was baffled. He never found out that for every shovel of coal that went into the train's fire, another went flying scattered into the fields in the darkness of the night.

In fiction much has been written popularizing

and romanticizing the Resistance man. But what was his real achievement? Perhaps his overall value is impossible to assess; but there is no doubt that his fearlessness and bravery were not only a great morale booster but also achieved very effective results.

The energy, time and cost of supplying the means of resistance was not misplaced. Resistance to any dictatorial or dominating force should be part of life, if only to preserve a nation's self respect. But it has to be carefully planned and there must be no egoistic heroics washing or weakening the movement. Let the free world be grateful to those who so courageously took such colossal risks; the many who suffered terrible torture at the hands of the inhuman Gestapo, and those who gave their lives with the result that most of the countries of the Western world have been able to retain their autonomy and individuality.

Surely the Resistance and the Maquis must have written one of the finest and most glorious chapters in the history of all warfare.

9

True Dutch courage

My admiration for the Dutch touches on awe and
wonder. They were brought to the edge of starva-
tion; yet they shared what little provisions they had
by feeding and hiding thousands of Jews, SOE
agents and many evaders and escapers. Mere words
cannot embrace the height, breadth and depth of
their sacrificial courage. When they sheltered
Allies on the run, they knew what awaited them if
they were discovered. A simple mishap or a chance
innocent remark by a child could bring imprison-
ment, lingering torture and eventually death. Their
homes would be burnt to the ground. Yet these
men and women went about their daily duties
showing little sign of fear, and accepting the
dangers with modesty and forbearance. Their
hearts were full of kindness and goodwill for those
who were trying to liberate them, and their devo-
tion was something not often seen in this materia-
listic world. It was a rare and beautiful thing. One
who experienced it at first hand was Graeme
Warrack, the divisional chief doctor of the 1st Airborne Division in the tragic Arnhem parachute
drop in September 1944. Hundreds were killed and
many captured. Warrack was one of the first to be
rounded up and soon found himself in charge of a
POW hospital set up to deal with the enormous
number of casualties. Escape was on every

prisoner's mind, even those who were quite seriously wounded.

Many plans were made for break-outs, all of which ended with the hope of finding a 'safe house' among the Dutch, whose hospitality had been given 'five star' rating long ago back in England. Many grateful escapers had been passed safely through Holland and returned to Allied lines during the previous four years.

Prized possessions among the hospitalized troops were items from the escape kits which my department had provided for all those going into combat. These were made of transparent Bexoid plastic through which could be seen a harmless array of chocolates, Horlicks tablets, a tube of full cream condensed milk, benzedrine tablets and a rubber bag for water together with water purifying tablets. Hidden among these items were an assortment of maps, compasses and small saw blades. They were hoarded in secret places around the hospital camp while escape plans were perfected. After only a few days at Arnhem, the Germans announced that a party of walking-wounded would be despatched to a hospital in the heart of the Fatherland. Warrack, finding that four officers intended to jump the train at night, told them to hand over their escape equipment. He then wrapped them in the smallest possible packets and stationed himself beyond the search parties. As the four officers passed him he wished them each 'God speed', slipping the packets to them as he shook their hands.

Warrack realized that he too would be transported to a POW camp in Germany as the number of his patients began to shrink. He began to give a little thought to his own escape. In a dark cupboard built into the bedroom alcove, his torch revealed a trapdoor in the ceiling. The cloud of dust that descended as he pushed upwards showed years of neglect and disuse. Beyond the trapdoor he found a plumber's inspection area. But how to get in without leaving behind a suspiciously-placed chair?

The doctor's solution was to fix a shelf at waist height across the cupboard to take his wash basin, soap and shaving kit. He then inserted two sawn-off screw heads into the bottom of the trapdoor, giving the impression that it was securely sealed shut. If this ruse failed, his own weight would hold it down should an inspection be made when he was on the other side of the trapdoor and a curious guard be tempted to try it. Finally, he arranged with his medical officer, who also wanted to escape, that they should both disappear the night before the planned evacuation of the remainder of the hospital. The Germans, they hoped, would conclude that they had gone together, and patrols would be alerted to look out for a pair on the run instead of one.

The plan worked beautifully. After several nights, Warrack emerged from his cubby-hole to find the hospital camp deserted. He took a compass bearing and set off in the opposite direction to his medical officer. All went well at first and then his progress ground to a soggy crawl after a day-long deluge of rain. He struggled on for hours, wet and shivering, until he spotted a small house standing by itself. Peering through the window he saw two young girls preparing supper. Somehow he felt that this might be a safe house for him. He knocked and waited. As the door opened he took a deep breath and introduced himself.

'Come in,' smiled the older of the two girls. 'We are friends.'

The words sounded like an angel's, and Warrack staggered with relief across the threshold while one of the girls ran to fetch 'Poppa' – their father. During supper Warrack discovered that the family had been evacuated. There followed what the world calls a coincidence but what Warrack later described as 'divine planning'. He told them he was a Scot. They all exclaimed in unison that they belonged to the Scottish Church in Rotterdam. Warrack went on to explain that his grandfather and father-in-law were ministers in the Church of Scotland, and a great feeling of fellowship was created between them.

Poppa explained to Warrick that German troops often stopped at the house to ask for directions or for water, and he suggested that a safer place might be the family's 'spare room'. Warrack was rather puzzled when he was led out of the house, across the garden and into a nearby wood. He was even more mystified when his Dutch host stopped in a small clearing, bent to brush away some leaves and removed the top soil to reveal a small trap door. Below was an earthen cave, well-boarded and equipped, measuring several feet long, about five feet wide and deep enough to stand up in. Poppa explained that the family had hidden many Jews in the 'spare room' until they were able to be spirited away to safer parts of Holland or out of the country. Warrack settled himself into his new home and his host explained that his daughters would bring hot food from time to time until the Dutch Underground could be alerted.

The Underground movement in Holland, the *Landelijke Organisatie*, was divided into small districts each being autonomous and, for security reasons, having only emergency contact with other groups. There was no central administration. Underground helpers were known only by code names, and passwords were continuously changed to minimize the danger of betrayal by 'quisling' Dutch collaborators. The contact man for the area covering Warrack's hideout was away for several days and so the doctor had no alternative but to sit tight and wait. His Dutch hosts provided a royal diet, despite their own poor provisions, and allowed him out at night to take exercise. When the contact man eventually arrived there was another delay of forty-eight hours while Warrack's army number and other details were checked by wireless with London. A second Underground man then arrived, dropped into the cave and began to give the doctor a thorough screening – a sort of third degree with kid gloves. Warrack knew he had passed the test only when two Dutchmen arrived at dawn the following morning with a spare bicycle.

Riding in the fresh morning air was at once exhilarating and frightening. So far, Warrack had done everything by night and now, dressed in Dutch clothing, he was pedalling past German troops and convoys in broad daylight. Four hours into their journey, his two companions told him to stay where he was, and they disappeared into a forest. A few anxious minutes ticked by before two other Dutchmen rode up to him. He later found that he had been passed over to another Underground district; guides disliked contact with other Underground men in case they were recognized. At night fall, he was left at a forester's house where he joined another six evaders settling down to sleep. They set out the following morning on foot along a narrow woodland path to rendezvous with a van marked with a red cross. They were then taken to a barn near the Rhine where a boat was due to take them across to the Allied lines the next day. Inside the barn they found even more evaders who had arrived from all parts of Holland. They quietly celebrated what they believed was their last night of evasion. Tales and adventures were swopped – all of which dwelt on the courage and ingenuity of their hosts.

One POW escaper had travelled the breadth of Holland posing as a cousin of his companions and wearing a lapel badge bearing the initials SH (*Slecht Horent*) to indicate that he was hard of hearing. When asked questions by German guards, he had simply pointed to his badge and waited for his 'cousins' to come to his rescue. On numerous occasions he had been searched but nothing incriminating had been found on him. A woman courier had his airforce identification papers and other secret details of German forces and fortifications which he had managed to acquire. She had gone ahead to meet them at the next hiding place. Apparently, the Dutch used women as couriers because they could pass through the check-points with more freedom than men. The Germans did not regard women as dangerous, and if a guard did make things difficult, a woman could often use her feminine wiles to avoid being searched. If it came to the worst, and incriminating documents were found, the Germans tended to be more lenient with women.

All in the barn marvelled at the incredible security of their hosts. Not even their Underground companions knew how far they were going, or who would contact them for the next stretch of the escape journey. At change-over points, one set of

Underground workers would disappear and a few minutes later their replacements would arrive. This meant that if one Underground group had been infiltrated, other groups would remain unaffected.

The escapers and evaders spoke also of the faith and peace of their hosts, and most men in the barn produced English Bibles which they had been given. There was common agreement that the courage of the Dutch had its foundations in a sane and uncomplicated belief in God and righteousness. Many of the men had been included in the family Bible-reading and prayers when gathered together in the evenings. There is no doubt that the fortitude of many of the Dutch people originated from their grounding in biblical Christianity and an unshakeable faith in God. They not only read the Bible but put its teachings into daily practice.

Evaders also exchanged stories of the excellent hospitality given in safe houses. One explained that he had been given two bottles of cognac and caused quiet laughter when he then explained how the women of his safe house had spirited away the bottles and swopped them for more practical commodities like butter, bread and cheese.

One SOE agent recalled how he had had a dispute with one of his hosts. The man had taken colossal risks to rescue a 'downed' pilot, and the agent had told him not to do it again.

'You must not ask that,' the man had retorted. 'Soon shall we be free and it is to you British that we owe it most of all. The sound of your RAF flying has been music in our ears and it is the only thing that gives us hope. Many RAF men are buried in graves in Holland. They were men who did their duty. So also now I must do mine for you.'

A rescued pilot went on to tell of another conversation which demonstrated the gratitude of the Dutch for the RAF.

'Do you know the most effective way of killing a German here in Holland?' the man had asked the pilot. 'Any attack by us causes reprisals – ten Dutch men dying for every dead German. This is useless,' the man had explained. 'But one pilot with his bomber can kill more Germans and do more damage than the whole of the Dutch Resistance put together. So we work underground to get you pilots back to England with as much information as possible.'

The talk in the barn went on quietly until one by one the men fell into a restless sleep knowing that in the dark early hours they would be floated across to the Allies.

Or so they thought. The last lap of the escape journey turned into a fiasco. The Germans, for some unknown reason, had doubled their river patrols. The evaders walked into what looked like a prepared ambush. Some were shot and most captured. Seven got to the river and crossed to safety, while at the rear, Warrack and two others realized it was every man for himself. They turned and fled in the direction they had come.

Graeme Warrack felt he had no alternative but to retrace his steps in the hope of starting again.

Poppa was washing himself near the window when Warrack knocked. The Dutchman looked at him in surprise, but quickly donned his raincoat and led the doctor once again into the woods. This time they seemed to be going in a slightly different direction and Warrack began to wonder what was happening. He then discovered that this incredible family had two 'spare rooms', and the second was even bigger than the first. It was lined with metal sheets, well-equipped and had two other evaders already in residence.

It was many nights before the Underground were able to work out a new escape plan. Days stretched into weeks and Warrack began to teach himself Dutch. Poppa provided a Dutch New Testament and the doctor spent his days comparing the words with the English version.

'Follow me.' The order was Warrack's first warning of the second escape attempt. A Dutch man helped him and his companions out, and they walked for several hours before they were shown into an empty house, the owners of which were away visiting friends. Their guide left them with a warning to stay away from the windows.

Warrack and his companions did not know it then, but the Dutch had suffered many severe setbacks. This was not the first time that an escape route had gone wrong. The experience of Yorkshireman Richard Pape illustrates just one of the many tragedies that happened.

Sergeant Pape's plane crash-landed near Hengelo in Holland, not far from the German border and both he and a Scot, Jock Moir, escaped the German search troops. The Dutch Underground, on hearing that the two had evaded the enemy, sent out a woodcutter with a haversack of food to locate them. He guessed correctly that they would be hiding in a certain wood and, on contacting them, gave them directions to rendezvous with a Dutch patriot. Hours later, they were hiding in some bushes at the rendezvous point when a farmer passed by and pretended to call his dog using the pre-arranged whistle. After introducing themselves they were taken to a farmstead and were welcomed by the owner, whose name was Basselink. He bowed gravely and said, 'English friends, all will be well. My family is good Churchill Dutch.'

Pape and Moir were then hidden in haystacks for about ten days until an SOE agent came to collect them. They were dressed as Dutchmen with their ID cards sewn into the lining of their jackets (if caught, they could produce them to avoid being shot as spies). They then cycled to Zutphan, entrained for Amsterdam, and eventually arrived at the home of a city businessman who accommodated them like kings.

The final stage of the evasion was to take them to the coast where they would be picked up by a boat. On the night of departure, fog descended and they had to return to the safe house. But the hitch had been observed by a Dutch Nazi, and in the early hours of the morning the German SS arrived in force. The Dutch businessman and his wife were arrested and sentenced to death while Pape and Moir were taken to a POW camp in Germany. It was much later that they learned that their hosts' sentences had been commuted to the slightly less horrible fate of a Nazi concentration camp.

With this sort of past experience, the Dutch moved Warrack and his friend through Holland as though they were valuable pieces in a life-and-death game of chess. They plotted each move with precision, always mindful of security, and progress was agonizingly slow. They were moved to a doctor's house which Warrack found most interesting. They then spent some days in the home of an English woman who had lived in Holland all her life and whose husband was the wealthy director of a shipping company in Rotterdam. The next stopping-off place was with a poor farmer. It was here that a German soldier barged into the kitchen where they were eating demanding to know the whereabouts of the farmer. Fortunately, they kept their mouths shut and thumbed towards the milking shed.

There were many similar hair-raising incidents as the trio were slowly moved west over Holland to the River Waal, south of Sliedrecht. Once again they reached the last and most dangerous stage of their journey, and for this they boarded canoes. They faced a twelve-mile journey down the wide River Waal, which was flanked by German searchlights and machine-gun posts. They manoeuvred quietly, keeping among the tall reeds that grew in abundance at the river's edge. When the searchlights swept in their direction they back-paddled to a halt so that the movement of reeds would not give away their position. Every so often when passing dangerous places, the Dutch would stop paddling and allow the canoe to drift silently with the tide.

The agonizing voyage stopped and flowed until the River Waal met the River Maas to form a broard estuary to the sea. Then followed a quick dash across to the southern mainland of Holland and to the safe harbours of Moerdych and Zwaluwe where the British forces were in occupation. Graeme Warrack stepped ashore to safety, four long months after escaping from Arnhem.

He later discovered that hundreds of Arnhem troops had been hidden by the Dutch Underground. There were so many to be harboured that the Dutch gave their last crumbs to feed our men. Our SOE had sent bombers over to drop food, money and equipment to help the Underground. Arnhem was the first advanced landing against the Germans in Holland.

From then on, other branches were formed to help the Allies as they prepared to liberate the country. The *Nederlandsche Binnenlandsche Strijdkyacht* (NBS) was established, to create small Dutch secret forces to hamper and sabotage German movement. Prince Bernhard was the mainspring of this movement, and our SOE were very much involved, training Dutch agents to act as wireless links between the NBS and the British Second Army.

One Dutch NBS unit known as 'Poppe's Group' spent three hours sniping at Germans around Flushing, after which some of the group decided to take a tea break. Poppe himself went to his nearby home for a rest. Not long after his return his wife suddenly whispered: 'Look outside!'

Coming towards the house was a high-ranking German officer. Poppe hid his rifle behind the door and calmly walked out.

'You had better shelter in my home,' he called out. 'There are a lot of snipers ahead.'

The officer thanked him and entered. Poppe immediately seized his hidden gun, took the officer prisoner and relieved him of his papers. They revealed that the officer had orders to blow up the docks and wharfs of the main shipyard. He turned out to be a Captain Lieutenant Blessinger, second in command of the harbour. Needless to say, the docks were left intact to await the British arrival.

During the occupation of Holland, 144 Dutch SOE agents were landed or dropped in their homeland. They had been taught to handle dinghies in the icy waters off the North Devon coast, to operate wireless sets and to use firearms at our Baker Street headquarters. Their targets had been moving cardboard effigies of Hitler. They were also taught to jump from moving trains and vehicles in such a way as to make difficult targets. When delivery by plane was impossible, the agents were taken by motor torpedo boat which could skim over the North Sea at fifty knots thanks to their three Rolls-Royce Packard engines. Of the 144 agents delivered to Holland, only 28 survived the war.

In the winter of 1944-45 as we forced the Germans to retreat, the Dutch in the Hague, Amsterdam, Rotterdam and Heer areas were starving. They dug up their precious bulbs for food. As soon as their plight was realized, we began to make emergency plans. General Eisenhower suggested to the Germans that supplies should be dropped and a conference was set up. General Bedell-Smith represented the Allied cause and General Von Blaskowitz appeared for the enemy. Seyss-Inquart, Himmler's deputy, also turned up. Dropping zones were agreed and to ensure that the drop was successful Bedell-Smith warned Von Blaskowitz and his senior officers that if there were any interference they would be tried as war criminals.

'As for you,' he turned to Seyss-Inquart, 'You will be hanged anyway.'

'That leaves me cold,' the Nazi retorted.

'That's exactly how it will leave you!' replied Bedell-Smith.

Queen Wilhelmina of the Netherlands was magnificent during the relief operations. She flew with her daughter and two Resistance men and installed herself in a small villa at Anneville although the German SS were only a dozen miles away. She concerned herself immediately with the hunger and desperate plight in which the Germans had left her people.

Prior to the war, the Queen was one of the few

realists in the Netherlands' governing authority who realized the true nature of Hitler's Germany. When her country was invaded, the Netherlands Commander-in-Chief informed her that she would fall into German hands if she stayed a minute longer. She left, and the next day she was blasting fiery salvoes at the Germans from Broadcasting House in London. She set up her headquarters at Chester Square Mews, and any Dutchman who escaped from Holland to England to join the Resistance had priority over all other interviews with her.

She had little time for Stratton House, the seat of the Dutch Government in the UK, which she designated 'Enemy territory'. Chester Square 'judged everybody solely on his or her record in the fight against the Germans and whoever in our opinion fell short we dismissed contemptuously.'

In exile, the Queen yearned to be identified with the suffering of the people – to be part of them. She wanted nothing of the past with its highly formalized and class-conscious surroundings and the selfish, fossilized Dutch government in London. A new era had dawned for the Queen. The old pomposity and formality had died with the invasion. The Stratton House types had returned to their pre-war gaiety, with sparkling lights and gaudy uniforms, while the forgotten Resistance fighters bicycled home in the evening on their home-made wooden tyres. The Underground hero who had risked his life countless times under occupation was left out in the cold by the Stratton House hierarchy; but to every true Netherlander, the exiled Queen offered her hand in equality and warm friendship.

The goodness shown, the generosity given, and the great risks taken by so many of the Dutch in helping our men to evade and escape cannot be praised too much. Only fools and barbarians glorify war. Aggressive war is a beastly and depraved business and fighting an aggressor is a sad and uncomfortable job, as our troops have rediscovered in the South Atlantic. But it has to be done when there is no other alternative.

What a contrast there was in Holland, between the Nazi vileness and the simple decency and human warmth of those who helped our evaders and escapers!

10

Comforts for troops

A successful escapologist needs two things: a knowledge of the tricks and techniques of his trade, and also the right equipment. The same was true for a POW who wanted to go 'AWOL' – 'Absent without official leave'! It was MI9's task to assist as many prisoners as possible to absent themselves without the leave of their German warders – and CT6 was fully involved. My 'Comforts for Troops' title was no mere cover for our more secret work. It was a genuine description of much of our business. We helped to equip and set up intelligence schools to educate soldiers and airmen in the art of evading capture or escaping once arrested. We went to great pains to demonstrate the range of gadgets and equipment and other 'comforts' available.

Group Captain John Whitley was one of our star pupils. He was one hundred per cent evasion and escape-minded and always flew his sorties fully prepared for any mishap. All manufacturer's labels were removed from one of his lounge suits, and he wore the trousers together with a civilian shirt under his uniform. He stuffed a tie, cap, razor, and other items into the pockets of the jacket and then rolled it up into a parcel which was constantly attached to his parachute. His air crew would wisecrack and grin at the precautions taken by their padded leader, but it was Whitley who had the last laugh. They were inevitably shot down over France during a bombing mission and only he managed to escape capture, returning to England via Spain with remarkable speed. Whitley, who later rose to Air Vice Marshall, had a few things to teach MI9 and our department on his return to England. While sheltering from German search troops he found tiny, telltale 'Made in England' labels on his shaving-cream tube, brush and matches. He had spent hours scraping off the give-away signs and, after his tip-off, we followed suit. By the time pilots were regularly flying over enemy territory we were supplying all items with French or German markings on them, which I had had specially manufactured.

In the early days of the war, I managed to get Bryant and May to produce a thousand French match boxes for SOE use. It was a fiddling, aggravating order for such a big mass-production firm, the more so because the boxes had to be perfect reproductions. But they graciously, even eagerly, agreed to help the war effort in this way and were happy to rush through my order. A week later MI9, having seen one of the boxes, rang Bryant and May to order 500. I 'lit up' with anger when I heard of this unnecessary duplication and immediately rang the Director of Military Intelligence and explained in colourful terms how such actions hindered my relations with firms and hampered the war effort.

'For security reasons,' said the director, adopting a patient tone, 'each secret department must not know what the others are receiving or doing.'

Before he had a chance to trot out the 'careless talk costs lives' war cliché, I fired back, 'Well, in that case, your precious security has broken down twice in one week.'

The director promised to note my annoyance and also my suggestion of a simple inter-departmental order system which I insisted would increase security, efficiency and reduce time wasting for my firms, myself and other secret departments. The idea apparently filtered up to Winston Churchill because shortly after this 'C', head of MI6, and the three directors of Air, Naval and Army Intelligence were brought together to form a 'Y' board and duplications like the Bryant and May affair ceased.

This mix-up had not been an isolated incident. A similarly ludicrous situation arose shortly after the RAF 'escape kits' had gone into full production. I was asked one day to come over to the War Office to join a conference of officials from the Ministry of Food and other departments. I walked in to find them anxiously examining my 'ration boxes', as the escape kits were code-named. The chairman explained to me that an MI9 officer had contacted him after an American had ordered an immediate consignment of the boxes and contents. The committee had already spent hours discussing production and had eventually rung Halex to see if they could take on the job of the boxes. Fortunately, they were put through to Mr. McKenzie, my contact there, who promptly told them to ring me. As their explanation came to a weak and weary standstill, I began to gather up the box and its contents and, as sternly as I could, I said:

'Gentlemen, I have all this in hand. This is still on the top secret list.' The expression on the officials' faces told me I was making my point. 'First, please forget what you have seen. Secondly, tell the American contact to get in touch with me. Thirdly, it is up to you to deal with the MI9 officer who let this out of the bag and caused this fiasco.'

I later learned that the MI9 man in question had wanted to impress his American counterpart by demonstrating what pull and influence he had.

Despite these unhelpful hiccups, our production of escape and evasion equipment went reasonably smoothly. One man who found the escape kit useful was RAF navigator Stan Hanson, who baled out over Holland at the end of 1944 between Winterswijk and Groenz. He wrote later:

In my battledress top I had two useful items of equipment: an escape kit and a silk map of Western Europe. The escape kit was contained in a perspex box six inches long, four inches broad and an inch deep, made in two parts and sealed by strips of adhesive tape. The underside of the box was concave and fitted neatly either over the breast bone or round the calf of the leg. It was incredible what they managed to pack into that small box. It contained twenty Horlicks malted milk tablets for sustenance, four Benzedrine tablets to ensure sleeplessness should the need arise, a fishing line complete with hook, a rubber pouch for storing a small supply of fresh water, a needle and thread wrapped around a card, a phrase card with a list of most apposite phrases necessary in French, German or Dutch, and a compass no bigger than a button, with north marked by two phosphorescent dots on the needle to cope with just such an emergency as I now found myself in.

The silk map resided in a small brown waterproof wallet. Only one piece of this assorted array was of use to me at this point in time. I could not read a map in the dark, neither had I the slightest inclination to stand chewing Horlicks tablets in the wet chill of a winter's night. But that little compass was vital. In their wisdom, the authorities had evolved a system whereby the kit was packed with the compass right side up, close against the perspex so one could read it without opening the box.

I had not checked my kit in any way, so I withdrew it now from my battledress, hoping that the packer had done his job right, and was ready to heap curses round his distant head if he had not. The thing *was* right! Through the perspex of the box I could see the phosphorescent dots marking north quite clearly. I held the box steady for a moment, took my compass reading and went off in a south-westerly direction towards our lines.

After a day and night of walking and hiding, frequently almost walking into German troops, Hanson decided to risk calling at a Dutch farm. He struck lucky, and was hidden in a smelly poultry coop until contact could be made with the Dutch Resistance. A bundle of old clothes was brought to him – a pair of old corduroy trousers, an old raincoat to cover his battledress blouse and a cloth cap topped his transformation into a farm labourer. He was wearing our special CT6 flying boots, and a knife soon separated the stitches holding the gaiters to the shoe part. He was left with a pair of ordinary walking shoes. The Dutch Resistance eventually smuggled him back to our lines.

The manufacture of our escape equipment and secret gadgets eventually involved hundreds of firms all over the country. One firm made shoes with secret compartments in the heels. Another threaded minute flexible saws into shoe and boot laces. They made an excellent tool for an agent or escaping POW when a nail was inserted at either end for handles. I also had manufactured a special type of rolled fibre which could be worked into the seams of uniforms or ordinary clothes. The fibre could be picked out of the material and unrolled to provide a writing surface measuring two centimetres across. It was quite handy for agents not possessed of photographic memories. Other firms 'doctored' all sorts of ordinary household items for me. Toothpaste tubes, shaving and hair brushes, shaving sticks and razors, torches, pens, pipes, cigarettes and lighters, were all ingeniously altered to accommodate maps or compasses. I still have a collection of the original articles, complete with hidden compartments, in my personal museum.

Maps and compasses were the most essential requirements for our lads on the run, and their design and production was given long and serious thought. It seems that in the Falklands War two of our pilots made a forced landing in South America, and had not been supplied with maps and other evading equipment, in order to know whether they were in Argentina or Chile. They wasted days finding out, and might easily have walked into Argentina and captivity.

Our maps had to fold down to postage-stamp size and be almost as thin. They were concealed in the fire-proofed bowls of tobacco pipes, or sewn into hems and lapels. One group of boffins and their firm created a special map which looked like ordinary plain white material (for example – a handkerchief or shirt tail) until an agent soaked it in his own urine. The backroom boys also came up with tablets to purify and reconstitute an agent's own urine so that it could be reconsumed. The concoction might not have exactly pleased a connoisseur's palate, but when you were dying of thirst, it had its usefulness. Our maps were normally reproduced on special non-rustling rag tissue paper in all sizes from eighteen-inch down to three-inch squares. These could be put flat inside the lining of a jacket or folded and used as shoulder padding. Alternatively, they could be folded and rolled round a fine needle, wrapped in water-proof jaconet and secreted in a shaving brush or the dummy cell of a pocket battery.

Thermos flasks proved useful hiding places for maps. In World War I things were hidden between the outer casing and the replaceable thermos bottle. This was too obvious for World War II. I decided to try to have a map inside the walls of the vacuum bottle itself. To cause the vacuum a chemical agent is inserted, the bottle sealed up, and thus the air is absorbed. But it was found that the agent also deteriorated the map and rendered it useless. After a month's experimenting, a non-destructive agent was found.

My firms excelled themselves when it came to compasses. Escape was impractical without these and we made it possible for a man to have several different versions hidden about his person. Almost anything could be fitted with a 'whizzer', as I coded them. We even magnetized fountain pen clips so that, when removed and placed on a pin, they would whiz round to point north. A razor blade or diamond shaped piece of metal suspended on a length of thread could perform the same task. We managed to conceal hundreds of these in puzzles, musical instruments and games which the Germans allowed into POW camps during the war. We had a nice line in removable gold teeth, hollowed out to house a miniature compass. False pen tops and signet rings were good hiding places but perhaps the most well-used was the fly button whizzer. We made one and half million of these metal fly buttons which could be separated into two halves. The top piece had a raised point in the middle which fitted into a depression in the lower piece so that it could swing round freely.

The idea for one of our most enduring compasses came while I sat day-dreaming in my CT6 office. It was during one of those rare 'cease fires' in the everyday blitz of telephone orders, callers and top secret memos. I was staring at a rural scene hung on the office wall, lost among ruminating cows. There gradually dawned a great longing to be away from the futility of war, to be back in North Africa on my pre-war farms, and the ones I used to manage for the Moroccan royal family. The cows drifted out of focus and I was again witnessing the magnificent Arab stallions flashing across the stud paddock in ferocious battle line. It was the spectacular 'Powder Play' when richly clad horsemen, waving sparkling muskets, galloped flat out towards the Sultan and his guests. There was the extraordinary thrill of this express army thundering towards you, then the volley of muskets, and the incredible sight as the horsemen reigned up their steeds on hindlegs only feet away from the stage. As I thought of the stud farm my wandering mind acrobatted illogically to another kind of stud.

'Of course!' I exclaimed at the static cows who remained quite unmoved by my genius. The yell of discovery had that 'Eureka' quality and I was up on my feet and pacing the office. 'Just the place to hide a compass! Why didn't I think of it before?'

Within days a prototype collar-stud compass was ready for trials. In its refined and completed form the stud had a black cellophane back. When

132

swivelled round, the luminous needle of the compass could be seen through a transparent 'V'. The background was also black, so nothing could be detected by even the most inquisitive of guards.

One of the men who used the collar-stud compass was New Zealander Lieutenant Roy Natusch who, after being captured in Greece, was put to work on a prison farm in an Austrian village close to the Hungarian border. One evening late in November, Natusch astonished his fellow inmates by announcing that he was going for a walk – to Budapest.

'You're crazy,' one prisoner diagnosed. 'Even if you escape you've got 150 miles of snow, blizzards and ice to get through.'

It was unanimously agreed that he would freeze to death before he reached the border. Natusch replied by showing them his compass, escape equipment and rations, and before another avalanche of protests descended he said a quick farewell and departed. His escape from the lightly guarded farm quarters went as planned and his stud compass guided him across the border and well into Hungary, a country officially allied to Germany though still neutral. His long walk to freedom ended abruptly in a wood on his fifth night out. He had risked a small fire to brew a cup of tea. In the middle of this task he looked up into the unmistakable muzzles of a battery of shotguns. At the working end of them was an unsmiling group of farmers.

Natusch gave himself instant promotion to captain knowing that it would carry more influence and attract better treatment. He introduced himself as an escaped British Officer from the New Zealand Expeditionary Force. The farmers, unimpressed and still suspicious, marched their prize to the nearby garrison town of Szombathely where an

English-speaking Hungarian lieutenant examined his escape equipment and story. This time Natusch obviously made a good impression for his next interrogaters were a colonel and then, astonishingly, two high-ranking government officials. For this last interview he had been taken in secret to Budapest.

The diplomatic preliminaries revealed that the officials were pro-British, very definitely anti-Hitler and scared to death of Stalin now that the tide was beginning to turn on the Russian front.

'We need your help badly,' one of the officials suddenly announced with an intensity that barely covered his embarrassment in having to ask. 'It is vital to our country's welfare that British and American forces land at the head of the Adriatic and along the Yugoslav coast and join up with Tito's guerillas. Will you stay and assist us?'

Natusch felt that he had little alternative but to agree. He was told that an Allied mission would fly to Hungary and land on a secluded estate. His job would be to supervise a suitable strip and give the necessary landing signals. On three separate nights Natusch stood by, ready to light the flares, with a car nearby to take the mission to a secret meeting place for discussions. But on each occasion the flight was put off at the last minute. Unknown to Natusch or the officials, political skulduggery was being planned in Europe's power corridors. Hitler had invited Admiral Horthy, Regent of Hungary, to Berlin to discuss the Russian advance, and while they were dining, on March 19th, 1944, German Panzer forces, led by the Führer's elite Blackshirt corps, swept into the country from all sides taking over key positions along with Nazi sympathisers living in Hungary. The Gestapo quickly rounded up

Natusch and his men, no doubt betrayed by a pro-Nazi Hungarian, and once again Natusch felt that it was time to go for another walk. He cleverly escaped from his captors and headed for the Yugoslavian border with the aid, once again, of his collar-stud compass. The Gestapo reacted quickly to his escape. Soon, alerted troops encircled him in a copse. He noticed a fallen tree with no leaves on it, devoid of all cover, and an idea began to develop in his mind. He lay alongside the trunk and then camouflaged himself using the dark cloak he was wearing. A few minutes later one German trooper, anxious to claim the reward for finding him, leapt over his cloak without giving it a second glance. Natusch waited until the searchers passed on. There were obviously other troops looking for him between his present position and the border, so he headed back to Budapest and went into hiding. During the following months, he had many incredible near misses, evasions and escapes, but by September 1944 he was again back at the Yugoslavian border. This time, couriers took him into Yugoslavia where he was handed over to a sergeant belonging to Tito's forces. There were fifteen other British escapers together with a large number of civilian recruits under the sergeant's command. Those who could shoot were supplied with rifles, which Lieutenant-Commander Gerard Holdsworth, our SOE man, had dropped from a base in Italy. This motley force hid during the day and moved forward at night towards the mountain fortress where Tito was installed.

German patrols were everywhere. They ran into one enemy unit in the course of the first night and many of their party were killed. Eventually, after passing through Marburg, Fiestritz, Chilli, and

Littai, they reached the Tito stronghold of Seisenberg. Natusch was there given a travel pass so that he could reach Semic, not far from an air strip used by transport planes to bring in arms for Tito's forces. After a few days he reached the landing site only to find it water-logged, and spent a week anxiously waiting for a plane to risk a landing. A Russian aircraft did eventually arrive and weapons and ammunition were quickly unloaded and wounded partisans put aboard. Natusch jumped in, the engines roared and the plane charged along the strip spraying great cascades of water to either side, just managing to clear the end of the runway before setting course for Italy. Natusch lay on the plane's metal floor, and fell asleep with his stud compass still operative and safe despite many searches.

I considered that work with MI9 was a priority to the war effort. Pilots and experienced fighting men were in such desperate demand that it was well worth the time and energy expended to help them to evade capture or to escape and rejoin the war.

In the initial stages of both World Wars, we had men expensively trained who were invaluable as fighting men. But we failed to train them to evade capture or to escape, and how to infiltrate back to 'fight another day'.

The education programme we launched after Dunkirk laid great stress on the psychological effect of capture. We hoped that prepared minds might be able to combat the boredom that eats the fighting heart out of so many POWs. We taught them what to expect on capture – an ever-increasing sense of hopelessness and lethargy as the enemy force marched them, always keeping them tired and hungry. Once behind barbed wire, frustration, impotency and utter loneliness, isolated them from all that was held near and dear. Then came the unbelievable boredom of a purposeless existance, eroding the mind and soul until prisoners degenerated into walking dead. We impressed upon pilots and troops the need to continue the fight; to wage war with their wits in the absence of their weapons. They had to be made to realize that they were still in the war; that for every thirty escape-minded and active prisoners, twelve Germans had to be kept away from the front line to guard them throughout a twenty-four hour day. Also, should they escape, it would mean that hundreds of troops would be kept busy tracking them down.

It was to this end that CT6 worked, and tons of escape paraphernalia were smuggled into POW camps during the war. We avoided using food parcels sent through the Red Cross. No risk could be taken with these badly needed goods which supplemented the minimal German rations. Instead, we secreted escape equipment in those parcels containing non-essentials, such as games, musical instruments and cigarettes. I had cotton-thin wire, with a breaking strain of 300 lbs, wound round cigarette tins and then rolled up underneath the lips at top and bottom. This wire was used for making flexible escape ladders. MI9 called me in one day to suggest do-it-yourself methods of covering the scent of fear left by all escapers. German tracker dogs were having too much success, and our POW's needed remedies. We managed to come up with quite a few ideas that played havoc with the dogs' smelling apparatus. Wild garlic, which grew in profusion in many parts of Europe, could be rubbed on the soles of an escaper's boots. If that was not available we suggested an occasional sprinkling of pepper which we began to send in 'non-essential'

137

parcels. We also included deodorants which the camp escape committees then collected, concentrated and distributed for use in boots before escaping.

It always gives me a great thrill to meet those who were issued with, or had used, my secret gadgets. I was holidaying in the Western Highlands of Scotland in recent times when I came across another tourist locked out of his car. He showed great excitement when I produced old escape-kit equipment from my car and used it to break into his vehicle. He introduced himself as John Carrick of Glasgow, who had served on the escape committee of the Lansdorf POW camp in Upper Silesia. He dropped me a line a few weeks later filling out some of the tricks of the escapologist's trade.

On each squadron there was an intelligence section where any operational airmen could obtain escape equipment – fine flexible saws and the like. These were sewn into our battledresses in collars and cuffs, and even intertwined in boot laces in our special flying boots. This boot had a detachable top and when the stitching was cut all that remained was an ordinary laced shoe.

Button compasses were obtainable which were sewn into trouser flies or on the blouses of our battledresses. There were several types of magnetic compasses, small traditional types with brass bodies and compass points with a glass cover. Everyone had his own idea of hiding them. Some were in hollowed-out heels of boots, others in belts or in chewing gum packets. If you were enthusiastic about escaping you could have the normal battledress altered to accommodate attachable accessories, like side jacket flaps and lapels. These turned a battledress into a civilian jacket. Lectures were given by intelligence officers, and, on one occasion, by a POW who had been returned by a French escape organization. Advice was given on methods of obtaining rail tickets and food coupons and also on the type of person to approach, depending on the country in which you landed.

Some prisoners at the beginning of the war managed to bring into camp some of their escape material. Usually, they were button compasses and maps. In Lansdorf there were 1,000 RAF personnel, who formed a camp within a larger camp. The main camp contained 30,000 British, Indian, and Allied troops who were divided into working parties and went to various factories and farms around Silesia. To get out of the camp one arranged a swop of identities with an army private and took his place in the working party. From there one could walk away to arrange railway tickets and food coupons. This sounds simple and occasionally was, but it was all backed up by planning and reconnaissance beforehand. Before leaving, compasses and maps were passed around on request. Several ingenious methods were used to copy maps, one of which was a series of wooden arms like a modern spirograph game, which could reduce a large scale map on to a sheet of toilet paper.

One of the most escape-minded men of the last war was Sidney 'Timbertoes' Carlin. He always went into battle fully prepared though he never had the chance to use his armoury of gadgets.

He had been a pilot in the Royal Flying Corps during the First World War and had a score of thirty seven enemy aircraft to his credit and MC, DFC and DCM after his name. He lost a leg in a flying accident but remained fully active, managing a large farm in Kenya and captaining a famous polo team out there.

When the Second World War began, Carlin was determined to fly again, despite his forty-five years and his peg leg. He travelled by dhow from Mombassa, but the boat sank in a Red Sea storm. He managed to swim ashore and made his way to Egypt and from there to England. With much tenacity and bullying of authorities he eventually became an air gunner. He had been a first-class marksman of big game in East Africa and he was in his element as a tail-end Charlie. He went over Germany in several successful operations.

His only 'prang' happened, not in the air, but on an English country lane. His car collided with another vehicle and Timbertoes was thrown out on to the side of the road. When he regained consciousness his first thoughts were for his missing wooden limb, and he shouted to his rescuers, 'What about my leg?'

His wooden leg was eventually found in the wreckage. It had broken open and spilling out of the insides were maps of Germany and France, compasses, files and hacksaw blades and a variety of emergency rations. A determined escaper's complete set-up!

11

Ssh! I spy. . .

Security, like chips, went with everything. It was first and last in every thought and action. Secrecy had to be maintained no matter what the cost or circumstances, and for four years it became natural to think at least half a dozen times before allowing the brain to engage the tongue or limb. My main item of luggage when I ventured out into industry was a wad of Official Secrets Act forms. Each new contact was shown the dotted line, handed a pen and ordered to sign. Even after this, the contact was given only the barest information beyond specifications needed to manufacture a required product.

It was only in recent years that I learned how successful my dire security warnings had been. I contacted many of my wartime firms asking if they could supply examples of their secret productions for a display that was being staged. I had the originals in my own personal collection, but felt that if loaned, they might be damaged or lost. All the firms wrote back saying that they were unable to oblige. Apparently they had been afraid to keep samples of secret work in case of a security leak.

Security was endowed with an almost godlike concept. You were to love it with all your heart, soul, mind and strength.

'Walls,' the security bible assured us, 'have ears!' This profound cliché was so well known that every wall in Britain must have heard it at least a dozen times a week. Beds were another inanimate security risk – or, to be more precise, what was under them. Post-war Britain had its 'reds' in residence under every mattress but we had our 'Jerries' – the human variety, of course.

The only haven of safety I had was my CT6 office – bedless, and with walls which were regularly 'de-eared'. I was doubly protected by an outer office and a secretary who gave an excellent imitation of a stone wall when necessary. My walls were fine. It was the door in them that almost proved my undoing.

The episode happened in August 1942. Sir Cecil Weir, Director General of the Ministry of Supply, was on one of his rare, impromptu 'walkabouts', chatting with the lower-archy. I was tucked away in my office poring over newly arrived, double-sided tissue maps of Mediterranean countries in readiness for 'Torch', our North Africa landings. The maps were for the SOE agents I had been equipping for their cloak-and-dagger runs between Gibraltar and the coasts of Algeria, Tunisia and Morocco.

Sir Cecil had apprently stopped off in my outer office chatting to my secretary. He had abruptly ended the conversation and marched straight into my inner sanctum to wish me a brisk 'Good Morning'. His sudden appearance placed not only my cover in jeopardy, but also the secret of the landings. He knew, as did others, that I supplied escape and evasion equipment to MI9 but he had no knowledge of my more clandestine operations with other branches. I had a split second to react. I could take him by the arm, frog-march him out, and give him a lecture on security and good manners. But as a minor MOS minion I somehow felt that this might not be the best way of handling it. Another option was to sweep everything out of sight. But this would merely arouse suspicion and would spark off one of those tedious boards of enquiry into just what was happening in CT6. I could confess all, but the repercussions of sharing the secret of the 'Torch' three months before it was due to be lighted, and then the added security risk of having MOS know my true work, was too horrible to consider. I did the only thing possible.

'Good morning, sir,' I smiled in reply. 'Come and have a look at these.' He crossed to my desk and picked up the maps.

'Beautiful,' he mused. 'I have never seen such fine and excellent tissue.' His eyes and fingers examined them with intense interest. Then came the inevitable question.

'Oh, they're for our POWs in Morocco and Algeria, sir.' The white lie came out uncomfortably. It was true that I was supplying maps for our North African POWs but certainly not the type that Sir Cecil was now examining. These would have been next to useless in a prison camp. I then switched his interest to some harmless escape gadgets. After a few minutes, Sir Cecil made to leave. I impressed upon him that his five-minute entertainment was for his eyes only and under no circumstances must he talk about what he had seen. Immediately he left, I locked the office door. It was my first and last security lapse.

My contacts in industry, having been sworn to secrecy, were delighted with their undercover role, even though they had no idea how their products were to be used. Hardly any of them let me down, although one firm tried it on one occasion. It was a tobacco company which was not so much bothered about keeping my secrets as its own.

Marshall Tito and his Balkan guerillas, one of my main customers in the middle part of the war, were desperately in need of all types of supplies and materials. They were doing a marvellous job resisting the combined might of German and Italian forces who were pressing down into Yugoslavia. Tito's men created so much trouble that they tied down several enemy divisions and hampered Hitler's thrust on the Russian front. Had Germany been able to forget Yugoslavia, hundreds of thousands of troops could have been diverted and the Russian front might have ended up in Alaska! One of my priorities was to keep Tito's men happy, and among one of the chief morale-boosting needs was cigarettes – Balkan cigarettes.

The English variety, if found on a partisan, would have signed his death warrant, so I sent out soundings among my contacts for a supply of Balkan tobacco leaf. After fruitless weeks, I began to experiment with imitation or synthetic substances until one patriotic tobacco lady eventually spilt the 'leaves'. She informed me that a tobacco company, one I had already approached, had a large supply of the required tobacco hidden in a country warehouse. The firm's directors were apparently waiting for the war to end so that they could make a commercial killing while their competitiors struggled for raw materials. In my fury, I telephoned Scotland Yard who immediately went into action. Within hours they had swooped, and two days after the tip-off the confiscated tobacco was in production. Fortunately, this firm was an exception to the normal patriotic rule.

Many of our top secret signals to Tito's forces had to be routed through the espionage-ridden Cairo, and a shiver ran up my spine when I read in my copy of the *Western Morning News* ex-corporal Jim Butcher's account of wartime security in that city. It had all the ingredients of a Whitehall farce, though SOE and our agents were honourably aquitted. Jim Butcher, now a journalist, wrote:

We paid scant attention to the artificial restrictions of phrases like 'secret', 'top secret', and even 'officers only'. I typed 'officers only' letters to other branches of GHQ – they were opened and filed by other corporals and private soldiers. In fact, the words had very little meaning. Possibly within G branch (which controlled operations in the desert) they might have been a little more strict. . .

One of my jobs was to preside over the ceremonial burning of the Eighth Army Order of Battle. This was a second document – 'officers only', of course – issued periodically and contained the title and strength of every fighting unit in the desert. It was undoubtedly a piece of paper Rommel would have prized greatly because it would have told him the exact strength of the formations facing his Afrika Corps.

It carried the injunction: 'To be burnt after reading' and with a box of matches, I used to stand in front of the kindly middle-aged colonel, with whom I worked, and set light to it.

This vital piece of paper was in my hand quite long enough for me to have made a copy in shorthand. I could then have walked out of the gates into the teeming multitudes of Cairo and disposed of it to the highest bidder. Of course, none of us did. Such action would have been unthinkable.

A few weeks after Rommel had stormed across the Western Desert almost to the gates of Cairo itself, an orderly from the Black Watch came into the outer office where I was duty corporal, and handed me a letter franked: 'Top Secret' and 'officers only'. I knew that the officer sharing my all-night vigil was an extremely short-tempered individual who would not relish being woken at 2.00 am, but who was very punctilious about those missives sealed with wax enclosed in two envelopes and franked in red ink with those so-called security devices. He had only just arrived from England.

'I don't know whether I ought to wake up the duty officer, Jock,' I said.

'Och, I shouldna bother,' replied Jock cheerfully, 'it's only about an invasion of North Africa next October. There's nae hurry aboot that.'

Where there was tremendous security was in the world of the SOE 'cloak and dagger boys' who used to disappear for weeks on end into the Balkans and elsewhere. I was strolling one night past one of the huge villas which had been commandeered. From an open window on the top floor there floated a message in morse code. It was obviously in cypher and, although I had been trained as a signaller in the Devonshire Regiment, and could do a respectable fifteen words a minute, it meant nothing. I told the colonel, who was then my boss, when I arrived in the office the next morning, and it was as if I had lit the blue touch paper. A sergeant from the Special Investigation Branch questioned me at length and I believed honestly that if I had been unfortunate enough to understand that message I would have been summarily disposed of there and then.

On the broad security front, where the lives of thousands of men were at stake, security was a Cairo joke. One general, so it was rumoured, was sent home in disgrace because his wife had exclaimed in a petulant voice, while lunching at Groppi's, that it was extremely tiresome that she and her husband would not be able to take a fortnight's leave because there was 'some sort of flap' due to take place in the desert.

Every day an army of several hundred Egyptian cleaners and labourers invaded GHQ. They were paid 50p a week, less the slush money each and every one paid the heroin addict who was their 'rais' or foreman. These men roamed everywhere. Technically, they were only supposed to do their cleaning under the eagle eye of a British soldier, but I never knew one case of this being checked.

One curious sequel. For days a small army of soldiers patrolled the streets around GHQ picking up scraps of paper some of them barely charred. They were the remains of a huge rooftop burn-up of all GHQ's non-essential files. Nearly all of them were marked 'Secret', 'Top secret' or 'Officer only'.

This independent evidence of SOE's excellent security in Cairo, compared to that of the army, confirms the experience I had of SOE in London and the tight security of their HQ and elsewhere. I firmly believed that the example of SOE in security matters so influenced the high-ranking officers of the Allied forces that they were able to bring this into use when planning the extraordinary security necessary for our D-Day landings.

While lower ranks scattered secrets like confetti, the high-ups could find security a suffocating affair. Winston Churchill often felt himself a 'victim'. Once, while in Casablanca shortly after the Allied landings in North Africa, he asked to be taken to see the *Jean Bart*, pride of the French Navy. Security threw up their protective arms in horror pointing out that he would have to travel through the native quarter and, in his war-weary state, he might pick up a disease. Churchill rebelled and told them to make the necessary arrangements, promising to be fit after a good night's sleep. Security, conditioned to rebellious charges, countered by pointing out that, as the Prime Minister was to be with Roosevelt at the Casablanca Conference, he might bring back a disease to the President.

Churchill replied that he was too old for those pastimes associated with the native quarters, but if he did forget himself and pick something up they could rest assured that he would not pass it on to the President. Security were not amused and the Prime Minister eventually lost his argument.

Those responsible for his welfare had other problems to consider. Casablanca was a spawning ground for spies, especially with the conference about to take place. They had already run into Germans and Vichyites. On one occasion Allied direction-finding apparatus hidden in a couple of old trucks had picked up short-wave signals which were traced to the Medina of Casablanca. Two British agents in Arab dress, with their apparatus strapped under their arms, took over the tracking in the narrow, congested passages of the old town.

Their aerials were concealed in the loose folds of their jellabas and head gear, and connected to a small plug in the ear. The two, linked by walkie-talkies, approached from different directions and the signals grew louder as they converged on the Bordel area. One of the agents approached a cubicle and a young girl sitting in the doorway looked hard at him but gave him no sign of invitation. He pushed past the girl and, as his eyes adjusted to the dimness, he saw what appeared to be a large woman sitting in a dark corner. She was covered with a veil and jellaba. She could have been any age – the girl's mother or a friend. She shifted her position a little and as she did a tiny trail of wire fell from the folds in her jellaba. The young girl started pulling the agent to the bed and simultaneously the huge bulk of the squatting figure arose and lunged at him. He felt a strangling grip at his throat and he realized these were the hands of a man. The agent's companion, who had reached the entrance, sprang forward, slammed the door to, and quickly garrotted the 'woman' and then the girl. The false bosom housed the transmitting apparatus and the two men quickly gathered it together and concealed it in their own robes. There were no tell-tale bits left behind beyond the two contorted bodies. The cost of security in this case was two enemy lives – but it could have saved the lives of hundreds of Allies. Our triumph in the security war helped lay the foundation for our final victory.

We had our Scarlet Pimpernels spiriting away thousands of prisoners and evaders along well-organized pipelines which were webbed across Europe. An evader in the heart of the continent could almost pick his escape 'package tour'. He could take the long, scenic route home through

Belgium, France, into Spain and across to Gibraltar to catch a cruise home to England. Those who went in for the rugged life could head north through Holland, Denmark and Norway and into Sweden. Exotic tastes were catered for through Greece into Turkey and Egypt. We also had the excursion routes which ran from Brittany to Helford in Cornwall, and for those with a sense of history there was a favourite embarkation point from a cove in France, thickly bordered with that rather rare plant – the scarlet pimpernel.

Britain's first 'pipeline' travel agency was set up by James Haydon Langley. He had escaped after being captured at Dunkirk and had headed south, returning to England via 'The Rock'.

MI6 gave him an office in Broadway next to my building with orders to help others emulate his escape. He was later joined by Colditz-escaper Airey Neave, the minister who was later assassinated by IRA terrorists, with a bomb placed in his car in the precincts of the House of Commons. I was often brought in to provide necessary escape materials. Jimmy Langley and I used to rendezvous at Southampton Row, Room 900. Some pipelines inevitably grew from Langley's personal escape route. Guides would bring in their 'parcels' through the Pyrenees, charging various stamp duties, depending on the time of the year and the danger involved. These guides, usually Spanish contraband men, gave us excellent service and we were happy to provide cash on delivery through our consuls in Spain.

Our ambassador in Spain, Sir Samuel Hoare, never did see the necessity of all this undercover work. Agent Denis Rake had completed a highly dangerous assignment with the French Underground when he decided to leave the country 'for health reasons'. With the Gestapo on his trail he was smuggled across the border into Spain. But having escaped from the French 'frying pan' he landed in the fiery oven of Miranda, a filthy Spanish internment camp. It was so bad that it made the German variety look like a Hilton hotel by comparison. Rake finally got an appointment with the British Ambassador and, after relating his story, Sir Samuel remarked 'I sometimes think you people are more trouble than you are worth.'

Jimmy Langley also had a frigid welcome in Madrid. Fortunately, this feeling did not extend to the executive people at the Embassy. On one occasion they showed remarkable efficiency and foresight in rescuing two high-ranking officers. The porter at the British Embassy received a small parcel addressed to the ambassador. Security officers were puzzled by the contents. Why should anybody wish to give the ambassador a half-used tin of Gibb's dentrifice? My office had had these circulated with a special compartment to carry secret messages and money of high denomination, and this eventually dawned on the security men. They found the following message inside:

> Brigade Major and self are hiding in a farm where six of us had Christmas dinner in 1939. Please send special guide and acknowledge receipt over French BBC broadcasts, incorporating the words 'sugar beet'.

The officers were soon identified by close relatives who could confirm the handwriting. Fellow officers revealed the Christmas-meal venue, which was just over the border in France. That night, the BBC broadcast the following reply:

> 'Worker calling for sugar beet harvest on

Monday.'

A guide collected his two 'parcels' and brought them back into Spain where they were returned to England via Gibraltar.

Belgian Doctor Albert Guerisse was responsible for establishing another escape pipeline after his country fell to the Germans. He himself had escaped in a British collier from a French port, and MI9 took him on, giving him the cover name of Patrick Albert O'Leary. The 'Pat' line returned 600 badly needed pilots and experienced fighting men to England. Airey Neave was one of them. His own pipeline, run with Jimmy Langley, brought back more than 3,000 pilots and aircrew, like Furnisse-Roe of Fighter Command, who used the service twice.

He crash-landed in Normandy in the autumn of 1943 and was back within three months. Eight weeks later he had to force-land his plane in France. As he unstrapped himself, he radioed to his squadron headquarters: 'Back in two months.' He was only a day or two late!

The quickest evasion in the war was that of a pilot who asked his French Underground rescuers: 'Can you get me to the church on time?'

Only five days before his wedding he had been forced to parachute into the grounds of a large chateau, owned by one of the French underground leaders. The romantic French were eager to help and squeezed him into an SOE airlift operation the day before the marriage was due to take place. The pilot arrived back safely to celebrate a double event!

As D-Day approached, up to a thousand of our aircraft were flying over France each day, seeking to destroy bridges, railway junctions and important roads. Escape pipelines were soon inundated as more and more customers baled out of their crippled aircraft. It became a major headache just to feed them, and this led to special sorties dropping a huge number of containers of food. Later on they had to be supplied from the air with arms, as the Allies advanced. Meanwhile my office was bombarded with orders for all the extra containers that were needed. America was fortunately able to supply the metal immediately, and my Mr Seager of the Metal Box Company, together with its subsidiary firms, quickly produced the goods.

All these escape routes had top-priority security. It was vital that we had an efficient, systematic escape network to recover our valuable men. Planes and materials we had. But we desperately needed the experienced pilots and aircrew to keep up the momentum against the enemy.

One of the main reasons why we were able to provide certain vital war materials and equipment was due to a little-known heroic undertaking by a thirty-nine year old bachelor, George Binney. It was also a victory for security considering the number of people involved.

CT6 was brought in to supply him with special life jackets, escape kits, self-heating tins of soup, and concentrated foods for the vital and dangerous enterprise of smuggling cargoes of ball and roller bearings and special steels from Sweden.

British industry was desperately in need of these raw materials when Binney contacted Sir Andrew Duncan who in 1940 was Minister of Supply. Duncan gave full backing to Binney's idea.

'It is of paramount importance,' he told Binney,

'that we receive all the war stores on order in Sweden. You must, at all costs, get them to England.'

Despite this clearance, the Admiralty forecast that the operation was impossible: the Skagerrak was blockaded by the German Navy; the German air strength was overwhelming and our Royal Navy was unable to give protection. They dismissed Binney's plan as an impractical, though novel adventure – but they failed to dissuade its author. Binney had had wide experience with the Hudson Bay Company in the Canadian Arctic, and then with the Norwegian and Swedish steel industries. At the beginning of the war, despite his first class knowledge of seamanship, the Admiralty turned down his application for a naval appointment because of his age. His tenacity and disarming ingenuity were now to take him to a goal far more interesting and important, thanks to Andrew Duncan's backing.

Binney arrived at the British Legation in Stockholm in June 1940 and, after explaining his intention, found himself once again facing stiff opposition. The British minister was against it, fearing political embarrassment because of Sweden's neutrality. The Admiralty attaché considered the operation impracticable, believing that its boats and their precious cargo would fall as free gifts into the hands of Germany. They also strongly suspected that the Swedish navy would interfere. A few months prior to this, we had 'arrested' four destroyers which the Swedes had bought from the Italians and which at that time had been harboured in the Faroe Islands during a storm. We feared that, had we not interned the boats, the Germans would have seized them and used them.

A fact, very little known, is that the Faroe Islands, which I know well, stood by us bravely throughout the War, faced considerable loss of shipping and supplied invaluable quantities of fish. I suppose only one person in a thousand knows what we in Britain owed to them in World War II. I have the highest admiration for these warm-hearted and indomitable people. They not only permitted our military, air and naval installations in their midst; but their ports, their mercantile and fishing fleets faced German bombing and sub-marine warfare.

When in April 1940 the Germans occupied Denmark, Winston Churchill broadcast: 'we are at the moment occupying the Faroe Islands, which belong to Denmark, and which are a strategical point of high importance. Their people have shown every disposition to receive us with warm regard.'

The four interned boats were soon released, but the Swedes were still angry. It was thought that they might use Binney's escapade to take their revenge. The British minister considered it would be wiser for Binney to drop the operation. Binney flatly refused to do this, and the minister then asked London to recall this rebellious bachelor. Binney had absolute faith in the operation. He scorned any form of defeatism and resolutely stood his ground. London eventually told the minister to give Binney full co-operation.

Five Norwegian vessels which had previously fled to Sweden were chosen by Binney. The owners feared for their loss at sea but a promise of full compensation was extracted from London. Yet another obstacle arose when the captains of the five boats considered that there was little chance of success and refused to allow their crews or themselves to get involved in such a suicidal mission. The obstinate Binney side-stepped this problem by travelling to Halsingmo where British masters and crews were interned yet with freedom of movement. His first recruit was a sixty-four-year-old ship's master, Andrew Henry, a disciple of physical and mental fitness. Henry was happy to be offered a trip home, despite the risks involved. Since his ship had been sunk he had endured long forced marches with no comforts and limited rations before reaching the safety of Sweden. All that he possessed was a hatbox containing his Bible. Being a religious man, he considered it the best thing to salvage. Binney surreptitiously signed up a full complement of captains and crews.

One last job remained. Binney had to be able to sink his mini-convoy quickly should the Germans appear on the horizon. It would indeed be a sad finale to let such a precious cargo fall into enemy hands. The solution came from Lloyd's chief surveyor who came up with an ingenious device. It was probably the first and last time that Lloyds had been asked to help scuttle ships!

Towards the end of January, the weather conditions became favourable – heavy snow falling making it impossible for enemy patrol boats and submarines to find them. The snow blizzard also immobilized the German air force. The small fleet crossed the North Sea until British aircraft and destroyers came to meet them, escorting them to Kirkwall Roads and the safety of British waters. The adventure brought freedom to fifty-eight Englishmen, fifty-seven Norwegians and one Latvian; also five valuable ships carrying a year's supply of raw materials for British industry.

The British minister, on hearing of Binney's success, recommended him for an MBE, but the government rejected that suggestion. They gave him a knighthood instead.

A second operation to bring out ten loaded boats from Sweden was organized for the long winter nights of 1942. This time the Swedish navy learned of the exercise and became as obstructive as possible. The convoy was delayed many times but eventually managed to escape into open waters. But they only managed to escape into the range of waiting German gunboats. Only two of the ten boats got through to England. The rest were either sunk, scuttled or had to limp back to Swedish ports. It was months later that British intelligence discovered that the chief of the Swedish navy was pro-German.

The indomitable Binney came up with another imaginative scheme – the use of fast motor gun boats called MGBs. They could pass through the Skaggerrak at night and be in the Swedish neutral territorial waters by morning. These boats brought a cargo of fuel, of which the Swedes were in dire need, and returned the following night, loaded with raw materials for our industry. From November 1943 to March 1944 these little warships, working from the Humber, brought to us 347 tons of vital precision supplies with the loss of only one MGB. There was only one human casualty and nineteen men were taken prisoner. This compared with the eighty-eight tons by air service, the shooting down of two Mosquitoes, two Lodestars and the loss of twenty-three lives.

When the Danes decided to set up a Resistance Movement as the Allies advanced through France, our SOE called on Binney. Three of his ships carried to Sweden 2,000 rifles and sten guns complete with ammunition, bazookas and rockets. This carefully camouflaged cargo was transmitted secretly to Denmark. The three ships returned to England with tons of special conveyor-band steel, obtainable only in Sweden. SOE, also through Binney's ships, supplied to Denmark through Sweden, large quantities of sabotage explosives, to cut off the enemy communications in occupied countries as we advanced.

It was not until Binney's death in 1972 that the Public Records Office released full information about the great work that he did. Sir Andrew Duncan, who had originally backed Binney, said, 'This operation enabled us to maintain our supply of ball-bearings until a vital new ball-bearing factory was put up. There is no need for me to exaggerate the importance of this operation.'

12

Not forgetting the workers

Those who produced my secret gadgets were, in their own sphere, just as dedicated as those agents who were dropped behind enemy lines. My craftsmen were dotted about London, some in large factories but many others in small two-man businesses. The latter struggled to produce my clandestine requirements in back-alley hovels, lean-to sheds or under railway viaducts. They often worked into the early hours with the bombs falling around them.

Their attitudes and dedication deserved a whole Honours List of decorations to themselves. They were a vital part of the incredible nationwide company which could be described as 'GB Unlimited'. No other country of its size and population became so organized and single-minded as did Great Britain in those dark, hectic days. Forty per cent of the people were directly involved in the war in one way or another, and a further five-and-a-half million were under arms. The extent of human mobilization was infinitely more than that of America and greater even than that of Nazi Germany. The British sumbitted willingly to every form of control. They also tolerated rationing longer than any other country, despite the fact that it was they who were the bulwark of victory.

The men and women who sacrificed much to equip our undercover lads have my special praise, and they will be a part of me for as long as I live. They worked unstintingly, often given no idea why a product was needed. They asked no questions and their vocabulary was refreshingly innocent of such phrases as 'demarcation disputes', 'wildcat strikes' and even 'office hours'. Without them and their dedication, SOE and other undercover agencies would have found it impossible to be effective.

The directors and craftsmen who supplied CT6's requirements were superb. They rose to my challenges with efficiency and sportsmanship, often amazing me with their speed and ingenuity. The secret of success, I found, was to get into the minds and motives of those with whom I did business. Each had a soft spot and personal reasons for helping. I then had to get over to them what I wanted. The first essential in all our equipment was simplicity. Secondly, the gadgets had to be durable enough to stand the repeated rough-and-tumble of field operations. Thirdly, they had to be easily dismantled or quickly hidden after use. Time was the fourth and most vital element. The deadline for delivery on many orders was often 'yesterday', and my contacts obligingly grew accustomed to this impossible pace.

'Leave it with us for a couple of hours,' was often the willing if weary reply. 'We'll have something for you then.'

Not all my suppliers responded so well. One or two directors proved awkward or inefficient, but only once was I forced to blacklist a firm – and that was for using inferior materials. I would often make several calls in a morning with only minutes to spare for each. The occasional director failed to grasp what was needed. A few others failed to concentrate on my initial specifications, and in those cases

I would tell them to have a rethink and ring if they made progress. I would then immediately contact another firm as a back-up. Lives depended on reliable, prompt service and delivery.

Workers could also supply headaches. Stoppages would occur, even over such trivialities as a tea break. But they were rare. Unions occasionally reminded management of their presence, complaining, for example, over their agreed rules being flouted. I remember one incident on my own doorstep when the hall porter rang to announce the arrival of a parcel. He was unable to bring it up to me, he blithely declared, because it exceeded the weight limit by a few ounces. It seemed somehow incongruous – there was this bone-idle porter squatting in his comfortable cubby-hole while some agent behind enemy lines anxiously waited for the contents of the parcel.

I went downstairs and the further down I went the higher my wrath rose. When I arrived at the porter's desk I found him sitting waiting for me. In fairly colourful language, I invited him to clear out and enlist with his friend Hitler – 'or perhaps your buddy, Stalin!'

I have never seen anybody move so fast as he moved then. Before I had a chance to finish saying all the things I had planned to get off my chest, he was taking the stairs two at a time, giving my parcel express delivery.

He was a rarity among the people I worked with. The vast majority would have accepted double their normal work loads if they thought that the nation would have benefited by it. In those days of the war, 'Mr Average' put himself in second place. For hundreds of thousands of men and women, the nation came first. They took enormous pride in the quality of their product, and efficiency, craftsmanship and reliability were acknowledged as virtues.

In today's world, the hard days of wartime sometimes seem like an industrial golden age. Today pressures of world competition, mass production, mindless jobs and soaring cost of living have all too often pushed the nation into second place and the ambitions of the individual to the fore. The virtues of quality, pride in one's work and trustworthiness are no longer to be taken for granted. Nor is it simply a matter of declining standards on the shop-floor; employers are often ready to sacrifice quality for quick profits, too ready to enjoy the benefits of factory ownership without having a proportionate commitment to the needs and satisfaction of the people whom they employ, and too ready to permit appalling industrial tension to develop when simple courtesy and consultation at an early stage might have prevented it.

The insatiable thirst for 'news' and the assumption by the popular newspapers that most people are only interested in conflict and tension, can easily lead to over-pessimism. But it is difficult to avoid the conclusion that there was an attitude towards work during the days when Britain stood alone against her enemies which is not so easily found in times of peace.

And 'peace' is itself a deceiving word. It is true that our nation at the time of writing has no immediate enemies, but we too easily dismiss the apparently minor inconveniences of neo-Nazism, the National Front, Communism and other movements of the extrme Right and the extreme Left. Even the Falklands War is as often seen as a demonstration of our security as of our vulnerability. In the face of all these, and such wider issues as plummeting world economies and incipient revolution, we are often too quick to assume that, like other crises in the past, these also will pass by us.

It is the weak conscience of apathy, and those afflicted by it choose to see and hear no evil. But they are dangerously mistaken. There is an enemy at our gates more treacherous than any we faced in wartime. That enemy is – self.

How many of our current problems can be diagnosed as, in essence, greed! Industrial unrest, social deprivation, rioting in our cities, tensions in the individual – all have at their heart an individual or a group wanting personal benefit at the expense of others. Perhaps saddest of all, the words 'patriotism', 'unselfishness' and 'the national interest' have in some quarters lost all meaning and are greeted with ridicule. Anybody using them is liable to be labelled a 'preacher', and disregarded.

As I enter my eighties, and ponder the changing values of our society, I believe I know which doctrine – that practised in wartime or that practised in peacetime – best profited nation and individual. The doctrine of 'self rules' is often heard today, but I never heard it in wartime. And so I find no alternative but to join the preachers.

But preaching can grow wearisome. The best sermons are short and to the point, and they are full of illustrations. My sermon has 300 of them. They are contained in my own personal 'Honours List' of heroes, many of whom were hidden away, far from glory and publicity, in back-alleys and lean-to sheds. In our hour of need, they came forward. Should the need arise again, their like would be found once more.

13

The Bomb!

The man's business card appeared innocent enough. And he had after all been directed to me through MI6.

'Tube Alloys', the card proclaimed, and the accompanying explanation from its owner sounded quite plausible. And yet there was something missing. A lot missing, in fact! For one thing, this man might be telling me the truth, but certainly not the whole truth.

'I need to contact some of your craftsmen,' he said, and the tone he used invited no questions. 'We have a small job on and we need to consult your experts.'

I had used similar opening tactics with my various contacts in industry, and it felt strange to hear them echoing back to me. Despite a certain nagging doubt, I had to confess that it was more curiosity than suspicion – I immediately obliged. MI6 had given the anonymous official high-level security clearance and I was in no position to refuse. My secretary typed out a list of craftsmen from my confidential pocket-book of contacts – men I had used on my own 'tube' gadgets, modifying bicycle pumps and producing special 'blowpipes' for use in field operations. At the time I had wondered whether another fiasco was brewing. Could somebody unknowingly once again be duplicating work I was already doing? I had to admit that this was not likely as the co-ordinating 'Y' Board was now operating efficiently. But why was industry now approaching me? Was 'Tube Alloys' indeed part of British industry – or was it, as I suspected, a commercial front for some clandestine Department of the Ministry-of-whatever? Of course, these questions were never verbalized. The game was not played like that. But it did not stop the queries making a mystery tour through the various recesses of my mind. My imagination did stretch to one or two likely solutions but when I eventually learned the whole truth I discovered that I had been as far away from it as one could possibly get.

It turned out to be my first encounter with 'the Bomb!'

The original work on the atom bomb was done in England by our scientists under the cover organization of 'Tube Alloys', which was established in the Autumn of 1941. It co-ordinated the work of the British atomic research teams, one of whom had delegated an official to enlist my help. Shortly after this enquiry it was realized that England did not have the industrial capacity nor the raw materials to develop the bomb alone. For a start, we would have needed hundreds of gallons of deuterium oxide (heavy water), half a million tons of steel and a massive industrial complex manned by a highly skilled labour force. With our factories and foundries already operating to full capacity, our key scientists were transferred to the States to join the atomic team being set up by Robert Oppenheimer. Churchill had previously visited Roosevelt and obtained the President's signature on an agreement to the effect that all research results would be equally shared between our two countries.

My second encounter with 'The Bomb' came months later. While America desperately worked against time to develop the A-bomb, our job on this side of the Atlantic was to ensure that the Germans did not. And the enemy already had a good head start on us.

Albert Einstein had written to President Roosevelt at the beginning of August 1939 concerning the possibility of an atomic bomb being produced – the first reference on record. It was known that the pre-war Germans had superiority in the field of nuclear physics, but then Einstein had fortunately emigrated to America and this had levelled the odds somewhat. The West realized that a man like Hitler could use the bomb to dominate not only Europe but the whole world.

This then was the starting line for the nuclear race, and Britain's priority was to destroy Germany's capacity to reach the finishing line. We knew that the Norwegian State Hydro Electric Board had established a plant north of Rjukan, seventy miles west of Oslo, for the production of 'heavy water', an essential ingredient at the research stage of atomic fission. The Germans occupied the plant even before the completion of their Norwegian campaign and immediately took steps to increase production.

Bombing the plant had to be ruled out. It would probably have proved ineffective, and might have killed many innocent Norwegians. Land-based assaults were to be tried first and, of course, CT6 was brought in occasionally for the more unusual supplies. The War Cabinet asked Combined

Operations Command to storm the heavy water factory and blow it up. SOE, especially their Norwegian section, strongly advised against the plan, but the War Cabinet went ahead. Thirty-four British officers and men went into intensive training and were then flown to Norway in two Horsa gliders towed by Halifaxes. Unfortunately, the aircrafts' magnetic compasses were affected by the ore-loaded mountains. The situation was compounded by adverse weather and the gliders crashed on to snow-covered rocky surfaces instead of landing on one of the flat strips twenty miles from the plant. Several men were killed, and most of the others were severely injured. All survivors were rounded up by Nazi ski patrols and, although in British uniforms, were shot on the direct orders of Hitler.

The SOE then took over completely. Ten men were selected for a second attempt – all of them Norwegian, including Jomar Baun who had worked in the 'heavy water' plant as chief engineer. The men were trained and equipped by SOE and also fitted out with my escape materials for use after the job was finished. These would be necessary on the long trek to neutral Sweden through the uninhabited snow-bound wilderness of hills and valleys. They had maps, compasses, torches, compressed food tablets and chocolate, and tiny watch-maker's saws in case a frost-bitten finger or toe had to be amputated. The team parachuted out of a black night sky at the end of February 1943.

The decision to use Norwegians was probably the biggest reason for the total success of the operation. And successful it was! The team penetrated the thick security screen around the 'heavy water' plant and brought production to a complete halt with their plastic explosives.

Norwegians at war were an extraordinary people. I began to suspect as much when my family and I were spirited out of Casablanca by our Norwegian skipper. Captain Stenersen calmly foxed the port authorities and then zig-zagged us safely home through waters infested with mines and U-boats. This had been his second 'escape', having previously sailed his boat out of her home port with the invading Nazis in his wake. I later learned with sadness that the SS *Varenberg* was torpedoed with all hands lost only months after landing us in England.

Frederik Aaran, one of our SOE radio men, typified for me the spirit of Norway. He was caught by the Germans in the act of transmitting details of enemy movements back to England. In the ensuing struggle, he was badly wounded in the leg, much to the anxiety of his captors. They had had orders from the Gestapo to bring him in alive and healthy enough to face their ingenious and inhuman methods of interrogation. The German troops immediately applied a tourniquet and left him to recover a little before transporting him to Gestapo headquarters. Aaran, realizing the motive behind their solicitude, refused to play the role of co-operative patient. Although racked with pain, he remembered that nearby was a knife that he had recently sharpened. Moving imperceptibly at first, his hand reached for it and then with the speed of a snake, he struck – plunging the blade into his own throat. Aaran's captors flung themselves upon him and soon staunched the flow of blood from what proved to be only a flesh wound. All was quiet again and Aaran lay still, pretending to be unconscious. But the Germans, in their panic, had forgotten to remove the knife. This time Arran made no mistake. He plunged the knife deep into his chest and cheated his Gestapo torturers.

Norwegians were men fortified with a rugged and deeply rooted evangelical faith in God and a righteous cause. They rarely spoke of their religion, and words like 'sacrifice' and 'idealism' were unspoken thoughts. They were men who preferred to express themselves through action. Their endless battling against the fierce Norwegian elements in everyday life made them well-suited to resist an enemy, to value their freedom and doggedly oppose all oppression. They were physically equipped for the kind of fighting war required and, being used to the capricious sea and the mountain storms, they faced death as naturally as birth and life itself. They were prepared to accept any ordeal. They feared not death, but only the thought that under torture they might give others away.

The Resistance movement in Norway, supported heavily by our SOE, played an important role in weakening Germany's armed strength. The German High Command had to maintain a disproportionately large number of troops – more than 400,000 for a population of less than three million – because of the constant sabotage, the fear of armed uprisings and the possibility of an Allied invasion. It was a time when the Germans were in dire need of reinforcements for the Eastern Front, and then later, after the invasion of France, the Western Front too. The Germans had a jigsaw of borders to patrol which, including the fjords, amounted to more than 10,000 miles.

Apart from 'heavy water', Norway had many

valuable minerals including pyrite at Orkanger, which was used in radar and wireless telegraphy. The destruction of these mines was one of our top priorities but they proved to be so heavily guarded that direct sabotage action became impossible. Eventually the power stations and pylons supplying the mines were blown up. Countless similar operations deprived the Germans of vital supplies, especially for aircraft production. There was widespread sabotage against harbours and shipping and the fearless Norwegian agents and wireless operators sent invaluable information back to England.

Gunvald Tomstad was a typical example. It was he who sent us the report that the *Bismarck*, Hitler's naval masterpiece and possibly the deadliest threat to our supply lines, had passed Christainsand heading west. This alert started the great hunt which eventually involved forty-two of our battle ships and aircraft carriers. Tomstad's incredible daring and intriguing deception, living in the midst of the Nazis and Quislings, deserves its own chapter. Miraculously he survived the war.

Our SOE sponsored 1,241 air sorties parachuting 12,524 containers and supplying more than 600 Norwegian SOE-trained agents and tens of thousands of Resistance workers with sten guns, bazookas, mortars, plastic explosives, limpet mines and millions of rounds of ammunition. Large supplies were also delivered by sea. At the end of the war, the Norwegian Underground had become so strong and disciplined that it was the only enemy-held country in Western Europe which liberated itself from the German invaders. The Nazis used foul and ruthless methods, even laying waste entire villages to stop resistance. More than 40,000 Norwegians were arrested, deported or imprisoned and more than 2,000 put to death. But in the end they proved too rugged and resilient for Hitler.

Much of the heroism of Norway came from her fishermen and merchant seamen who escaped after the invasion of April 9th, 1940. They returned many times to land wireless operators, agents and supplies in support of the Underground. They often sailed back to England with compatriots to be trained and, later, returned. The hazardous voyages were undertaken in their small boats, enduring some of the stormiest seas of the world. At one point early in the war they had lost forty per cent of their sailors engaged in clandestine work, and more than half of their boats, and were on the verge of giving up the battle. Admiral Nimitz, a Commander-in-Chief of the American naval forces, heard of their plight, and US navy submarine chasers were immediately dispatched from Florida. Three weeks later they arrived at the British Norwegian secret base in a small concealed inlet of one of the Shetland Islands. They were larger, faster and more luxurious than anything they had previously used. The American sailors who crewed the boats were highly amused to find that their Norwegian 'pupils' knew nothing of drill, saluting or the rest of naval etiquette.

The delighted Norwegians willingly accepted the boats and assistance in equipping them, but naval orders were another thing altogether. They believed that all men were born equal, and woe betide any officer who believed that he was more equal than they. What they lacked in naval etiquette, they made up for with courage and tenacity against a stretch of sea more cruel than most. The saga of the *Arthur* and her five-man crew provides more than enough evidence to prove this point.

Larsen, the skipper, with Sangolt, Bjornoy, Platten, and a new engineer Iversen, had an uneventful thirty-hour outward trip from the Shetlands, to land their two agents and a cargo of arms and explosives near Kinn. They then set out to return to the Shetlands but after ninety miles the wind came up and progressively increased to hurricane force. Sangolt volunteered to take in the mizzen sail and minutes later two enormous waves broke over the ship. As the *Arthur* shook herself free from hundreds of tons of water, her waterlogged engine spluttered to a halt. All hands set to, hand-bailing with buckets, and an hour passed before anyone had time to notice that Sangolt was missing. The mizzen sail blew as rags in the wind, but he had vanished. They never saw him again.

The engine was re-started, and the remaining crew spent the next four days and nights struggling to keep the boat's head to the sea. The slightest error of judgement could have broken the *Arthur* in two as she rose and fell in the sea of mountains and valleys. Larsen assembled all hands in the six-by-four-foot wheelhouse, where they sank to the floor exhausted. After a cramped twenty-four hours one of them fixed quarters in the engine room, reached by a small inner door from the wheelhouse. This meant that at least three of the crew could lie down and sleep, for none cared to cross the thirty feet of open deck to their bunks in the forecastle. A hole was also cut in the bulkhead to reach the galley. For a hundred hours the storm beat down upon them and visibility was never more than a few yards. The storm grew in intensity and they became weaker and less capable of holding the ship on course.

It must have been on the third evening that an enemy plane strafed them. They did not hear the explosions at the time. Only later, after the fourth day when the sea's anger was spent, did they discover several pieces of cannon shell embedded in the structure around them. When dawn broke on the fifth day they saw land. They realized that had visibility been better they would have been able to see the Shetlands all the time. The *Arthur* limped into her base with her mast lying in a tangle of rigging, the bulwarks smashed and everything swept off the decks. Below, it was even more chaotic.

These were the Norwegians – the type of men who probably saved the Free World from Hitler's atomic Reich. The operation on the only 'heavy water' plant in Europe was probably the most momentous raid in the whole of the Second World War. It enabled the Allies to win the nuclear race and bring the war to an end.

In the short term 'The Bomb' saved millions of lives – Allied as well as Japanese. The capture of Okinawa, for instance, cost the lives of over 100,000 soldiers on both sides. If the Japanese defended an island which did not belong to them with such ferocity, how much more would they have demanded in defence of their own mainland? Had the Americans been forced to bomb Japan as we blitzed Germany, millions more lives would have been lost or ruined. In cold statistics, the loss of Hiroshima and Nagasaki – horrible though these were – meant that dozens of other bigger communities and thousands of fighting men of both sides were saved. The two bombs preserved the lives of 200,000 Allied prisoners of war who would almost certainly have died if the fanatical Japanese had faced a prolonged defeat. The suddenness of the two bombs so took them by surprise that they surrendered. The shock and horror enabled them to salvage their national and religious Samurai pride. Otherwise many would have chosen to die in mass ceremonial suicides rather than be defeated.

I believe that in the long term, the bomb has gone on saving lives. Since World War II, several nations have fought each other with conventional weapons. The larger nations have often fought through the proxy of smaller nations, but on a world-wide basis it is the bomb that has protected us from another global confrontation. The more terrifying the nuclear bomb becomes, the less likelihood there is of it being used.

Mine is not, in many quarters, a fashionable view. 'Deterrence' is rejected in favour of 'Disarmament', and often even 'Unilateral disarmament'. I believe that, sincere as such convictions are, they are contradicted by history. Britain paid a terrible price in 1939 for her disarmament after World War I, and nobody knows what difference a strongly armed Britain might have made to Hitler's ambitions.

Of course there is great value in pursuing adequately-supervised arms limitation. Perhaps in that way energy and money could be freed to cope with some of the desperate needs facing the world's population. But I believe it to be utter foolishness to pretend that the bomb can be banned from our minds or our territories. Knowledge gained is ignorance lost. In the Garden of Eden it was the first lesson that mankind learned, and the first to be forgotten.

Whether or not we believe that story to be literally true does not matter in this context; the illustration is valid in either case. Adam split the forbidden fruit; we split the atom. In both situations, knowledge was gained and innocence irretrievably lost. There could be no going back.

That is why, I believe, the bomb can never be banned. We know about it and we have the technology to reproduce it. Nothing this side of a nuclear holocaust can erase that knowledge from the memory of the human race.

Humanly speaking – a bleak outlook! But, thank God, humanity does not have the last word on the subject.

14

Sand Dieu rien

The Universe is incomprehensible and man is a mere purposeless accident if there is no Creator. But if there is a God – and a recent opinion poll revealed that over eighty per cent of those questioned believed that there is – then how absurd that society should declare him to be an embarrassing taboo. Surely, he should be the Number One topic in the conversation of reasonable and reasoning men.

For those whose interests extend no further than our hidden heroes and the glimpse that they give into the back rooms of British Intelligence, my book is now at an end. I warn them to read no further. The extract above is taken from the pages that follow, and will serve as summary. The statement it makes is the only way I know of re-tuning the desperately pessimistic note that was sounded at the end of the previous chapter.

It is not customary for an author to dissuade his readers from finishing one of his books. He writes to be read, and I am no exception. But, equally, most writers aim for honesty and are averse to enticing their readers into unsuspected territory. Again, I am no different.

So read on only if you must.

Dozens of war films have made the scene immortal.

183

The country road; POWs being forced-marched on either side after being captured at the front; enemy troops and tanks hugging the crown and travelling in the opposite direction. Suddenly, out of a clear sky come the diving, strafing planes.

On one such real-life occasion, the prisoners were British. So too were the planes. They swooped, sending guards and prisoners alike diving for shelter behind nearby cottages. Bullets and shells whined around and into the flattened figures. And at the height of the attack a German trooper stood quietly on the back doorstep of one of the cottages.

In the echoing quiet left by the departing planes James Spencer, a hard-boiled British commando, looked up at the German. Spencer, crouching in a mud hollow, had noticed the trooper after the first wave of attacking planes. He wondered at his careless nonchalance, recalling that he had observed the same attitude in a few of his mates. What surprised him most was to see it exhibited by one of the enemy. Spencer challenged: 'You a Christian?' It was half statement, half question.

The guard nodded pleasantly: 'We're all in the hands of God.' He added: 'Living or dead it makes no matter.'

The war was seen rather differently through the opposing eyes of an English pilot who had been involved in many such strafing attacks. Roger Hall's book, *Clouds of Fear* has some of the most vivid descriptions of air combat ever written. He also writes of his fear and inner conflict over 'so much senseless killing'. At a time when he felt unable to continue, he heard the royal Christmas Day broadcast of that year.

'Go out into the darkness,' urged the King, 'and

put your hand into the hand of God, and that will be better than light and safer than a known way.'

This broadcast had a profound impact on everybody – believers and un-believers. It came at an opportune moment – especially for Hall.

P. R. Reid, one of the few who proved that Colditz was not escape proof, ends his book *Colditz: The Latter Days* with an American doughboy opening the gate to the inner prison courtyard:

> The prisoners rushed towards him. . . to make sure he was alive, to touch him and from the touch to know again the miracle of living. . . freed from bondage. . . their faith in God's mercy justified, their patience rewarded, the nobility of mankind vindicated, justice at last accomplished and tyranny once more overcome.

On the plane from New York to London many years after the war, my neighbours were two Thai students *en route* to a German university. War took hold of the conversation and they marvelled how tiny Britain had dared to face, alone and practically unarmed, the might of Germany. After a moment's thought, I suggested, 'I suppose we did it in the same way that David faced Goliath. David said: 'You come with a sword. . . I come in the name of God – the battle is the Lord's'.''

In the forties many in England had David's certainty – not merely a blind faith, but an unshakeable trust and belief that right would prevail. It was a faith in the fact that God rules, and righteousness and justice, no matter how black the situation, would ultimately triumph. Forty years later this sort of trust seems almost a relic of a bygone age. But without it life is emptied of purpose and man loses his direction.

Ian Fleming, who turned '007' from three digits

into a thrilling drama, was asked by a boyhood friend shortly before he died: 'Ian, what is it like to be famous? Ever since I've known you it's been what you really wanted.'

Fleming's face fell: 'Well, I suppose it was all right for a bit. But now. . .ashes, old boy – just ashes!'

Fleming saw himself on the treadmill of success, condemmed to pass his days acquiring wealth to no purpose and having little faith in anything. Talking of human success, he concluded: 'You've no idea how bored one gets with the whole silly business.'

When I was a young man in Paris, the French Admiral Dalencourt gave me his motto, *Sans Dieu rien* – without God – nothing! The universe is incomprehensible and man is a mere purposeless accident if there is no Creator. But there is a God – and a recent opinion poll revealed that eighty per cent of those questioned believed that there is – then how absurd that society should declare him to be a embarrassing taboo. Surely, he should be the Number One topic in the conversation of reasonable and reasoning men.

Not long after my talk with the admiral, I enlarged the motto by adding, *Sans Bible rien*. One of my wartime priorities was to ensure that every pilot or outwardbound agent had a map tucked safely away in a shaving brush, hair brush or whatever. Without the guidance of this map, a wrong turning would have been inevitable and capture certain sooner or later.

Biblical topography is the only authoritative guide I know in the warfare of life. Its sane wisdom is ever relevant for daily life and its principles help evaluate all things. Nor am I alone in this belief. Ord Wingate of Burma Chindits fame. Montgomery of Alamein and, more recently, General Moore, the Falklands liberator, read their Bibles each day, especially in battle. They readily attributed their success to its principles.

My second addition to the admiral's motto was *Sans Christ rien*.

The Bible states that man deserves to be separated from a holy God because of his self-centredness – his 'sin'. The separation is described as eternal death. Sin erects a barrier between us and God, just as it does in ordinary human relationships. We are trapped in a self-made dungeon of Colditz proportions called selfishness, and few seem to realize that an escape route was provided 2,000 years ago.

God loved the world so much that he sent his Son to demolish this barrier once and for all. Jesus Christ came and paid the penalty which we deserved for our sin. The innocent died for the guilty. Three days after his sacrifice, he completed his work by conquering death itself.

New Testament writer Paul explains it superbly: 'Death is destroyed! Victory is complete! Where death is your victory? Where death is your power? Death gets its power to hurt from sin. But thanks be to God who gives us the victory through our Lord Jesus Christ.'

The greatest escape of World War II came when Allied troops marched in to tear away the barbed wire. They routed the enemy and freed the captives. Christ did the same through his resurrection. He entered Satan's escape-proof prison of death and then came out. Those who are in Christ will also enter death, but with the knowledge of the escape route. They too will rise to new life. An unprejudiced examination of the evidence of the resurrection has changed many an agnostic mind. A former Lord Chief Justice of England once said that if the resurrection facts were ever placed before a British jury, it would have no alternative but to return a verdict that Jesus rose from the dead.

The essence of Christianity is that Christ offers freedom and his power in our lives to break out of the prison of our own selfish entanglements. James in the New Testament writes: 'From whence come wars and fighting among you? Is it not from your own desires?' Wars and battles between nations, within families and among individuals will rage on. 'There will be wars and rumours of wars till the end of time' – Christ's words. The only possible solution is for man to allow himself to be changed by God. Without this 'changing' or 'new birth', the fighting will never cease.

Realistically, we live in a world where selfishness reigns supreme. Where self rules, fighting will inevitably follow. Fighting is a fact of life. A Christian cannot bury his head in the sand and ignore it.

Nowhere in the Bible is the protection of one's family, or the fighting of a defensive, just war ruled out. The New Testament shows the absolute necessity for the enforcement of law and order, and of being armed for defence. Jesus Christ states 'When a strong man, fully armed, guards his possessions he is safe and lives in peace.'

Christ never told leading military men, such as the centurion, to lay down their arms. Instead he uses the centurion's position as an illustration. Paul also uses countless military similes to illustrate true mature Christian life. He stresses that the Christian life is spiritual warfare, and we would not be told to 'fight and endure as a good soldier' if the phrase was based on a wrong principle. Christ makes it plain, as in Matthew 24, that there will always be evil and war, and despotic and aggressive men and nations, until he himself comes to rule and reign in peace and justice. Until then, we are told to 'resist (fight) the devil and all his works', and that means the evil which exists in our personal lives and also in nations throughout the world.

If we sit back, evil will triumph as a matter of course. In the thirties complacency – the stupid 'Peace at any Price' complacency – brought upon the world a terrifying agony. Some today are seeking to lead us into the same ghastly situation, urging disarmament and defencelessness. Some would even trim away our police force; many think it a crime to use physical discipline on wrongdoers. They, in their näivety, are unwittingly encouraging bullies, despots and aggressive individuals and nations to take action. In a previous age this would have been classed as betrayal of family, country and biblical Christianity. Some pseudo-Christians rip biblical verses out of context to propagate a deceptive and unbalanced form of God's love. But God's love has given us his laws. If we allow these laws to be neglected and to be broken, chaos and fighting will naturally follow. We must be prepared to love God as he loved us, and to fully enforce his law and order.

We need to recover a strong but compassionate discipline in our homes. We need to strengthen our police force and to ensure that our military forces are capable of providing real defence. And this must include an adequate nuclear deterrent.

While man refuses to be ruled by the Prince of Peace he will remain cursed by his own folly. This is why we need to be fully armed, whether with sticks, bows and arrows, or nuclear weapons. Being armed is the only deterrent against future war, and the only thing that will give us any chance of peaceful co-existence.

If the free nations on this earth want to retain their liberty and way of life, they must overcome their individual lethargy and selfishness and act as one united force – fully armed. Such a deterrent, even though very costly, is far better than enslavement or the untold cost and disaster of another global war.

We must keep vividly in mind the words of one of our great generals, Oliver Cromwell who said: 'Trust in God and keep your powder dry.'

I also trust that our Intelligence Services (the 'Sinews of warfare') have the right men of the highest integrity and capability, and also the right tools for the job. They should have the facilities they need for the defence of this land and our people worldwide, for theirs is one of the most important jobs in our society today.

Napoleon wisely said: 'One spy in the right place is worth 20,000 men on the battlefield.'

This is just as true today.

'THE VICTOR IN WAR
IS HE WHO IS BEST INFORMED'

Abbreviations

BBC	British Broadcasting Corporation
BCRA	*Bureau Central de Renseignement et d'Action*
BIS	British Information Service (Washington DC)
CIA	Central Intelligence Agency (American equivalent of MI6)
CT1	Clothing and Textiles (Navy)
CT2	Clothing and Textiles (Army)
CT3	Clothing and Textiles (Air Force)
CT6	'Comforts for Troops' (officially Clothing and Textiles 6)
DMI	Director of Military Intelligence
DNI	Director of Naval Intelligence
GCCS	Government Code and Cipher School
LRDG	Long Range Desert Group
MEW	Ministry of Economic Warfare
MI5	Security Services
MI6	Secret Intelligence Service (SIS)
MI8	Distribution of Signals, Code School, enigma
MI9	Allied POW escaping, evading and life lines, Interrogation
MIS-X	American POW escaping and evading
MIS-Y	American interrogation of enemy personnel
MO1 (SP)	Cover name of SOE

MO4	Cover name of SOE Cairo
MOS	Ministry of Supply
NID (Q)	Naval cover name of SOE
OSS	American equivalent (1942) of today's CIA
PIU	Photographic Interpretation Unit
POW	Prisoner of War
PRU	Photographic Reconnaisance Unit
RSS	Radio Security Service
SAS	Special Air Service
SIS	Secret Service — MI6
SOE	Special Operations Executive
XX	Double-Cross Committee